DATE DUE		
FEB 21 1990		
OCT 2 199		
DUE 5H		
FEB 22 1993		
SEP 28 1993		
MAR 20 1995		
FEB 16 1999		
SEP 18 2003		
VIRL		
due: 12 May 11		

Jesus and Marx:
From Gospel to Ideology

by

Jacques Ellul

translated by

Joyce Main Hanks

WILLIAM B. EERDMANS PUBLISHING COMPANY
GRAND RAPIDS, MICHIGAN

Copyright © 1988 by Wm. B. Eerdmans Publishing Co.
255 Jefferson Ave. S.E., Grand Rapids, Mich. 49503

Printed in the United States of America

Library of Congress Cataloging-in-Publication Data

Ellul, Jacques.
[Ideologie marxiste chrétienne. English]
Jesus and Marx: from gospel to ideology / by Jacques Ellul;
translated by Joyce Main Hanks
        p.   cm.
Translation of: L'ideologie marxiste chrétienne.
Includes bibliographical references and index.
ISBN 0-8028-0297-4
1. Communism and Christianity. 2. Ideology. I. Title.
        HX536.E4313   1988
261.7—dc19   88-10203
                                                CIP

CONTENTS

PREFACE

At what point does a theology become an ideology? How can a Christian distinguish the two? Jacques Ellul has always taken pains to differentiate them, but in the present volume, published in France in 1979, he provides us with both a theoretical framework and important examples. Some popular theologies, particularly those that attempt to intertwine biblical theology with Marxist thought, fall into the trap of reaching "theological" conclusions by other means, Ellul believes, so that we cannot consider them as true theologies.

Such theological thinking merely follows the current sociological trend and serves to justify that trend by surrounding it with an aura of sacredness. Ellul has long fought this tendency of Christians to "bring up the caboose," finally tumbling to what is in vogue when the rest of society is ready to move on to something different. Christians should be in the forefront, he believes, showing the way and pointing out future dangers for the rest of society, rather than conforming to current tendencies and beliefs.

We could consider this book, then, as an additional example of an Ellulian constant. Mixing Christianity and Marxism fits the pattern of all previous Christian efforts at syncretism, in Ellul's view. But the significance of *Jesus and Marx* overflows such a formula, since the book deals at length with a number of Ellulian themes: revolution, Marxism, politics, anarchism, theology, freedom, ideology, poverty, etc. I will not attempt here to outline all Ellul has had to say on each of these important topics. We do need to observe, however, how Ellul's earlier works begged for such a volume as the present one, and, more importantly, how his recent writings tend to modify what he has written here.

Ideology and Revolution in Ellul's Early Work

As James Gaffney has pointed out, Ellul wrote on the relationship between Christianity and revolution long before the topic
began to attract any general interest.[1] By 1948, when Ellul's *The
Presence of the Kingdom* was published in French, he considered
revolutionary Christianity a key element of his thought. This
seminal book, along with the final chapter of his *Autopsy of Revolution*, outlined in tantalizing fashion the possibility of genuine
revolution within the Christian context.[2]

Ellul originally opposed much of the contemporary effort to
make Christianity revolutionary, however, since conformity to the
world's notion of "revolution" usually resulted. Indeed, one of
Ellul's main criticisms of the Church is its tendency to legitimize
and participate in movements with no real Christian foundation.

False Presence of the Kingdom was Ellul's first book-length
treatment of this subject.[3] In this early work he pointed out
many errors that are more fully treated in *Jesus and Marx*:
adapting to the world's thinking, claiming Christian motivation
for following sociologically determined trends, applauding the
Church's addiction to the "latest thing," automatically welcom-
ing outsiders' criticism of the Church, cooperating with them in
the Church's ruin, attributing ultimate value to politics, justifying political involvement through faulty exegesis, and substi-
tuting political activity for preaching the gospel, to mention a
few. In many ways, the present volume constitutes an updating
of *False Presence of the Kingdom* and an application of its principles to concrete situations and theologians.

In *Autopsy of Revolution* Ellul maintains that authentically

---

1. James Gaffney, "Jacques Ellul: A Christian Perspective on Revolution," in Thomas McFadden, ed., *Liberation, Revolution and Freedom* (New
York: Seabury, 1975), pp. 176-91

2. *The Presence of the Kingdom*, trans. Olive Wyon (Philadelphia: West-
minster, 1951); originally published as *Présence au monde moderne* (Geneva:
Roulet, 1948). *Autopsy of Revolution*, trans. Patricia Wolf (New York:
Knopf, 1971), was originally published as *Autopsie de la révolution* (Paris:
Calmann-Lévy, 1969).

3. *False Presence of the Kingdom*, trans. C. Edward Hopkin (New York:
Seabury, 1972), was originally published as *Fausse Présence au monde moderne* (Paris: Les Bergers et les Mages, 1963).

Christian revolution opposes current trends in society rather than joining them (the Church's habitual response, usually effected about the time the rest of the world moves on to something new!). This early evaluation of budding liberation theologies accuses them of mutilating Christianity in order to defend it against its foes: revolutionaries who accuse Christians of supporting the status quo. Readers familiar with the writings of Francis Schaeffer will sense an affinity between Ellul and Schaeffer at this point; such common concerns abound, although major differences between the two thinkers remain.[4]

Ellul came down especially hard on Arthur Rich, Richard Shaull, Jean Cardonnel, and others who he felt put revolution or politics first and their Christianity second. Clearly, as other theologians of this stripe surfaced, Ellul felt constrained to take them to task, finally combining several already-published articles with fresh material to form *Jesus and Marx*.

In 1968 Ellul introduced some of the criticisms of contemporary theology described at length in the present volume.[5] Ellul had insisted in *The Presence of the Kingdom* on the urgency of finding ways to communicate the gospel to modern people. Instead of concentrating on communication, however, the Church through the ages has often sought to make the gospel more palatable. Like Cain, modern theologians emphasize human horizontal relationships to the exclusion of the vertical relationship with God, Ellul feels. Thus God, no longer needed, can be proclaimed "dead," and humanity "comes of age" in new independence.[6]

Ellul provides some of the history behind certain political theologies in *Violence: Reflections from a Christian Perspective*.[7]

---

4. See David W. Gill, "Jacques Ellul and Francis Schaeffer: Two Views of Western Civilization," *Fides et Historia*, 13, no. 2 (Spring-Summer 1981), 23-37. Chapter IV and other parts of the present volume treat the matter of presuppositions, another key theme for both Schaeffer and Ellul.

5. See Jacques Ellul, "Cain, the Theologian of 1969" (trans. George Haskell Vernard), *Katallagete*, 2, no. 1 (Winter 1968-1969), 4-7.

6. See also Jacques Ellul, *The Ethics of Freedom*, trans. and ed. Geoffrey W. Bromiley (Grand Rapids: Eerdmans, 1976), p. 48n.15.

7. Trans. Cecelia Gaul Kings (New York: Seabury, 1969); later published in French: *Contre les violents* (Paris: Centurion, 1972). Ellul some-

Here he documents previous assertions that Christian justification of violence has a long history and is anything but a new development in the Church. As we will see, Ellul discovers later
that while violence may play a part in some liberation theologies, pacifism characterizes them more typically.

Violence also summarizes Ellul's ideas on poverty, an issue
which he believes forms the starting point for Christian ap-
proval of violence in the "theologies of revolution" (pp. 30ff.).
While sensitive to the needs of the poor (defined broadly to include many who are not in physical need), Ellul decries the reduction of current problems to just one: the unequal distribu-
tion of material things (p. 38).

In *Violence* Ellul characterizes "ideology" as a belief based on
pseudoscientific principles, with aims different from those it
states, and with a justificatory purpose (pp. 77-79). The present
volume both amplifies and illustrates this definition. In *The
Ethics of Freedom*, Ellul treats some liberation theologies briefly.
He denies that all oppressed peoples can be equated with God's
"chosen people," and insists that salvation extends beyond liberation through human efforts. The "new" theologies follow an
"ideology of revolutionary practice" and Marxist conformism
instead of carving out a genuine theology (pp. 425-26). Ellul
maintains that true liberation and revolution involve destruc-
turing society (p. 471).

Besides developing Ellul's intriguing notion of an authentically Christian revolution and his view of poverty and ideology,
the present volume elaborates on other earlier ideas: the reversal that takes place in the roles of oppressor and oppressed after
a revolution, for instance (presented in *Violence*). At the same
time, *Jesus and Marx* hints at ideas that will make significant contributions to subsequent books: language viewed as a prison for
children, and church history gone wrong.[8]

---

times uses "liberation theologies" or "theologies of revolution" to refer to
tendencies in the 1960s that are typically called "political theologies" in
the U.S.

   8. Ellul discredits the former notion in *The Humiliation of the Word*,
trans. Joyce Main Hanks (Grand Rapids: Eerdmans, 1985); for the latter
see his *The Subversion of Christianity*, trans. Geoffrey W. Bromiley (Grand
Rapids: Eerdmans, 1986).

Liberation Theologies in Ellul's Later Work

Often we fight hardest the source of our greatest temptation. For years I assumed that Ellul condemned our modern tendency to prefer efficiency above all else because he was naturally inclined in the opposite direction. A year of interviewing him made it clear to me that he struggles with his inner bent toward efficiency first of all—and only sounds as though this enemy comes at him from the outside. So it is, I believe, with liberation theologies and Marxism. Ellul often sounds so disparaging that we assume he is single-mindedly opposed to the objects of his criticism. We must remind ourselves that his struggle to live with one foot in Christianity and the other in a certain form of Marxism has not ended.

Following up Ellul's suggestion in *Autopsy of Revolution*, Thomas Hanks has proposed him as "the original liberation theologian."[9] Hanks substantiates this possibility, noting Ellul's concern for the poor, his dialogue with Marx, his use of the social sciences in doing theology, his dialectical thinking, his emphasis on the Exodus (as the paradigm for salvation) and on praxis, and his nonviolence.

We might conclude, then, that Ellul attacks the theologies of Georges Casalis and Fernando Belo in *Jesus and Marx*, not because they are so far removed from his thinking, but because they represent an error into which he might also have fallen. Theology converted into ideology is not a danger for others only. This hypothesis finds some corroboration in Ellul's comments on liberation theologies subsequent to the publication of the present volume in French (1979).

However strongly Ellul feels about errors in certain liberation theologies, he has always insisted on their importance, calling them "an essential trend in modern Christianity."[10] Thus, after a blistering attack on Casalis in 1978,[11] Ellul, as director of the journal *Foi et Vie*, welcomed Casalis as guest editor of the September 1981 issue (devoted to liberation theologies). In the

---

9. Thomas Hanks, "The Original 'Liberation Theologian'?" *Cross Currents*, 35, no. 1 (Spring 1985), 17-32.

10. "Liminaire," *Foi et Vie*, 80, nos. 4-5 (Sept. 1981), 1.

11. Jacques Ellul, "Les Idées fausses ne tombent pas du ciel," *Réforme*, no. 1741 (5 Aug. 1978), p. 7; expanded in Chapter VI below.

same "Liminaire," Ellul points out that since 1970 these new theologies have evolved, and in any case are often poorly understood.[12]

By 1982, Ellul had found some liberation theologians with whom he could agree; at this point his criticism of them as a group, if not muted, becomes at least more complex. In a long article Ellul reviewed four works on liberation theology.[13] He gives bad marks to Ernesto Cardenal's *Chrétiens au Nicaragua: L'Evangile en révolution* for a Marxist manipulation of the Scriptures and of simple believers, though Ellul recognizes Cardenal's sincerity. He also faults the volume edited by Julio de Santa Ana, *L'Église de l'autre moitié du monde: Les Défis de la pauvreté*, as mostly redundant and impractical, as well as riddled with errors (concerning the definition of the poor, the source of truth, etc.).

Ellul's review of two other books, however, is extremely positive: Thomas Hanks, *God So Loved the Third World*, and Vincent Cosmao, *Changing the World: An Agenda for the Churches*. He credits Hanks with establishing the importance of the biblical theme of oppression and its link with poverty, as well as the integral quality of liberation as promised in Isaiah and Luke. Concretely, he distinguishes Hanks's view of Jesus' praxis from Belo's. Ellul finds Hanks's theology different from the ideologi-

---

12. See also the "Liminaire" in *Foi et Vie*, 81, nos. 5-6 (Dec. 1982), 2, a second issue devoted to the theme of liberation theologies.

13. Jacques Ellul, "Quelques Livres de la théologie de la révolution," *Foi et Vie*, 81, nos. 5-6 (Dec. 1982), 75-89; reproduced with some modifications in *Les Combats de la liberté* (Paris: Centurion, 1984), pp. 145, 186-97 (see pp. 168-97 for an overview and update of Ellul's views on revolution, poverty, and liberation theologies; he includes a bibliography), the third volume of Ellul's *Ethique de la liberté*. The four books reviewed are: Ernesto Cardenal, *Chrétiens au Nicaragua: L'Évangile en révolution* (Paris: Karthala, 1980); Julio de Santa Ana, ed., *L'Église de l'autre moitié du monde: Les Défis de la pauvreté* (Paris: Karthala, 1981); Thomas Hanks, *God So Loved the Third World*, trans. James C. Dekker (Maryknoll, NY: Orbis, 1983; Ellul bases his comments on the original version, published in Spanish: *Opresión, pobreza y liberación* [Miami: Editorial Caribe, 1982]); and Vincent Cosmao, *Changing the World: An Agenda for the Churches*, trans. John Drury (Maryknoll, NY: Orbis, 1984; Ellul bases his comments on the French edition, *Changer le monde* [Paris: Cerf, 1981]).

cal sort of liberation theologies, such as those propounded by Belo and others mentioned in *Jesus and Marx*.

Finally, Ellul confesses he had expected to reject Vincent Cosmao's ideas when he first began to read him, particularly because of the pretentiousness of his title. But he found this new theologian truly convincing and valuable, in part because he first provides a sociological analysis, on which he bases his prescriptions for the Church's action. Ellul disagrees with certain details (such as Cosmao's preference for "inductive theology," based on praxis—an important theme in *Jesus and Marx*). Ellul finds that such theology ends in mere ideological justification, and he maintains that the scientific community has now condemned the inductive method. (Theologians would do well to catch up with them, he urges!) But he agrees enthusiastically with most of Cosmao's presentation. Ellul expresses special relief at finding at least two theologians who speak to current concerns without assuming only Marxism and violence can liberate the poor.[14]

In one of his most recent books Ellul makes it clear that only some theologians of liberation twist the biblical concepts he is concerned to defend.[15] He has consistently maintained, however, that many liberation theologies succumb to an ideological view that involves filtering Christianity through Marxist presuppositions.[16]

Since writing the different parts of *Jesus and Marx*, then, Ellul has followed developments within liberation theologies with great interest and care. Increasingly he distinguishes between theologians who seem to him to represent biblical teaching faithfully and those who put their Marxism ahead of their faith. If he writes sympathetically of the former, he continues to criticize the second group with no holds barred, as in this volume.

Readers are encouraged to take special note of the date of original publication for each of Ellul's previously published articles included here (provided in a footnote at the beginning of the

---

14. See Ellul, *Subversion of Christianity*, pp. 134-36.

15. Jacques Ellul, *Ce que je crois* (Paris: Hachette, 1987), p. 273n.1 (Eng. trans. forthcoming).

16. See Jacques Ellul, "L'Ambiguïté de l'Eglise des pauvres,'" *Le Monde*, 23 February 1985.

appropriate chapters). In this way, Ellul's stance can be appreciated within the context of the above overview as well as for its relation to current events. His tendency toward hyperbole becomes more acceptable when we remember the events and trends of the moment that he is taking pains to expose in the most forceful language possible. At an earlier or later date, his position on a given topic is often expressed much more moderately.

Belo, Casalis, and the Bible

In the French edition, Ellul called Chapter I of the present volume an "Overture," an appropriate title for the beginning of a book that combines a series of articles in symphonic "movements" to consider a single main theme from different angles. In this case I would label the theme something like "ideological and political interpretation of the Bible." The author takes pains to give us his own views as well as to criticize those with whom he disagrees.

Ellul approves and makes use of several hermeneutical methods. In a volume published in 1981, he states that the only inadequate approach in his view is the "materialist interpretation."[17] In *Jesus and Marx*, Ellul combats the materialist method and provides some examples of his preferred approach.

Readers who appreciate Ellul at his exegetical best will welcome his treatment of Matthew 9 in Chapter IV here, which to my knowledge has not previously appeared in print. Let those new to Ellul beware; in this chapter he makes use of one of his favorite devices: playing devil's advocate, that is, presenting the opponent's case with such good arguments that he all but convinces the reader. At this point he begins to tear down the adversary's position. Only after reading the entire chapter (or the whole book!) can one hope to state Ellul's position with any accuracy.

---

17. Jacques Ellul, *A temps et à contretemps: Entretiens avec Madeleine Garrigou-Lagrange* (Paris: Centurion, 1981), p. 166; Eng. trans.: *In Season, Out of Season: An Introduction to the Thought of Jacques Ellul, Based on Interviews by Madeleine Garrigou-Lagrange*, trans. Lani K. Niles (San Francisco: Harper & Row, 1982), p. 188.

Using Belo as an example, Ellul attempts to show the impossibility of a materialist analysis of the Bible (Chapter V). Jesus would remain outside the scope of such an analysis, even if historical knowledge were adequate for such an interpretation, which it is not, he contends. After several years, Belo chose to respond somewhat sheepishly to Ellul's criticisms.[18] He appears to consider some of Ellul's views seriously, but I find no trace of any change of heart in Belo's preface to the English version of his book.

Having dispensed with Belo's materialist interpretation, Ellul takes on the development of inductive and materialist theology (Chapter VI), singling out Casalis's book for attack. In the process, he addresses some of the questions posed by H. Richard Niebuhr.[19] When asked recently if he should be grouped with those who opt for "Christ against culture" or with those who see Christ as transformer of culture, Ellul preferred the latter designation, adding his affinity with the "Christ and culture in paradox" view.[20]

With the publication of *Jesus and Marx*, Ellul's most extensive study of anarchism ("Anarchism and Christianity," Chapter VII below) becomes generally available to English-speaking readers for the first time, in a fresh translation. Those who have been intrigued by hints of his unusual reasons for opting for anarchism will find his somewhat subtle stance spelled out here. Some readers may discover with surprise the vast difference between historical anarchism and the caricature often associated with it. An intellectually respectable position dating from the nineteenth century, it still has serious adherents today—but surely few who, like Ellul, view it as a means rather than an end! Teachers of Ellul's thought have long considered this article a classic.

---

18. See *Foi et Vie*, 78, nos. 5-6 (Dec. 1979), 121-27; see also Ellul's brief reaction at the end of Belo's comments (p. 127).

19. H. Richard Niebuhr, *Christ and Culture* (New York: Harper & Row, 1951).

20. Unpublished interview by Daniel B. Clendenin, trans. Jack Robinson, 24 April 1987, in Bordeaux.

Notes and Conclusion

In the pages that follow, I have frequently added biblical references (using the Revised Standard Version unless otherwise noted), as well as publication information and page numbers of books referred to, when these were lacking in the French version of *Jesus and Marx*. Readers wishing to locate Ellul's hard-to-find articles and books can request most of them from the collection on microfilm at the Wheaton College Library (Wheaton, IL 60187-5593).

Some readers may have questions about Ellul's expertise in the area of Marxist studies.[21] His lifelong interest led him to introduce courses on Marx and Marxism (at the university of Bordeaux) well before such studies became common. He continued to teach these courses until retirement in 1980. Although Ellul makes critical use of some of Marx's social and economic principles, his thorough knowledge of Marx and Marxist thinkers enables him to formulate such stinging criticisms that Marxists commonly reject him.

Never one to hold back when a principle is at stake, Ellul may have alienated more groups of people in this volume than in many of his other works. Most readers will find plenty to object to, but Ellul will stir them to reflection in most cases, and that is all that matters to him.

I have been able to find only a handful of reviews in French for this book. It is my hope that it will inspire many more now that it is available in English.

Joyce Hanks

---

21. See also Ellul's "On demande un nouveau Karl Marx," *Foi et Vie,* 45, no. 3 (May-June 1947), 360-74; *Propaganda,* trans. Konrad Kellen and Jean Lerner (New York: Knopf, 1965); *The Betrayal of the West,* trans. Matthew J. O'Connell (New York: Seabury, 1978); "De Karl Marx à l'Afghanistan," *Sud-Ouest,* 12 Feb. 1980; *Perspectives on Our Age,* ed. William H. Vanderburg, trans. Joachim Neugroschel (Toronto: Canadian Broadcasting Corp., 1981); "Encore une fois . . . christianisme et communisme marxiste," *Conscience et Liberté,* no. 22 (1981), pp. 10-22; "Un exemple de confrontation: Marxisme et christianisme," in Gabriel-Ph. Widmer, Jean Brun, and Jacques Ellul, *Les Idéologies et la parole* (Lausanne: Presses Bibliques Universitaires, 1981), pp. 53-72; *In Season, Out of Season;* and *Changer de révolution: L'Inéluctable Prolétariat* (Paris: Seuil, 1982).

Chapter I

Introduction

1. Christianity and Ideologies

"Ideology" has become a hackneyed topic for discussion, but it can mean just about anything. In common usage, it means "any opinion different from mine," always with an unfavorable connotation. If we look to specialists, we discover as many definitions as there are sociologists!

Let us begin with my definition, a kind of common denominator often used in specialized studies. This one has the advantage of relating concretely to the facts: an ideology is the popularized sentimental degeneration of a political doctrine or worldview; it involves a mixture of passions and rather incoherent intellectual elements, always related to present realities.

Today's political universe is littered with ideologies that make the practice of politics both easier and more difficult. They make it easier to manipulate the masses through propaganda, but they complicate decision making, since the ideological effect must always be taken into account. Anything can be labeled an ideology, just as anything can become one: Nationalism, Socialism, Liberalism, Democracy, Marxism, Anti-Racism, Feminism, etc. Often an ideology springs up to parry an ideology-free practice. Male domination, for example, has no explicitly formulated ideology; feminist ideology arises to oppose it. Capitalism is a practice with no explicitly formulated ideology; socialist ideology arises to oppose it. Afterward, capitalism will produce an ideology of "defense." Often an ideology strives with an outdated ideology: racism is still practiced but no longer has a genuinely ideological expression. But opposite it anti-racism comes to life—and it is thoroughly ideological.

Within this expanding ideological movement so peculiar to

1

our time, Christianity can clearly also become an ideology. In fact, it has become one. As faith, as God's revelation in Jesus Christ, as theology (searching to make faith and revelation explicit), as a practice that is *faithful* to God's will, Christianity is not an ideology. But it has become one, and relentlessly continues to become one, whenever it is a means for distinguishing those who are right from those who are wrong (the saved and the damned), a principle for life conduct and for directing the world, a Christian political construct, a will to convert at any cost in order to swell the ranks of a given church, a system for organizing society, or a moralistic system (teaching that behavior is objectively good or bad, according to a clear and timeless definition of good and evil). In any of these cases, Christianity is truly an ideology.

Each of these errors involves a degeneration: of theological doctrine into simplification, of faith into beliefs and feelings, and of the practice of freedom into mere religion. The blending of these three errors produces an ideology. This is a serious matter! Christianity was originally an anti-ideology! The very concept of revelation opposes ideology and Christianity (an "ism" [in French]—but it should not be!).

Two timeless principles oppose ideology and Christianity: (1) God's biblical revelation necessarily entails iconoclasm, that is, the destruction of all religions, beliefs, idolatrous images, and fads. We must bring this up to date and apply it to our current idols—Money, the State, Science, etc.—but also to religions like Communism and Maoism. Iconoclasm aims at everything ideological that tends to take the place of the revealed God. (2) On the practical level, the Bible reveals that all Christian conduct is founded on God's liberation. God does away with our alienation so that we can live as free people. Thus we must attack all ideologies, since they force us to conform, join us to an orthodox group, and sweep away our capacity for choice and individual reflection.

The agonizing difficulty in all this involves detecting ideology. If the Christian faith prepares us to ascertain ideology, where do we find it? Clearly the first step is to question Christian ideology itself: Christianity as power and as ideology. In this connection we see that Karl Marx's and Friedrich Nietzsche's criticisms, for example, are clearly on target. They question the ideological aspect of Christianity.

But it would be much better for Christians themselves to do this work. All we must do is get on with criticizing our own ideas, convictions, churches, and movements on the basis of a demanding rather than a rationalizing reading of the Bible. This means we must renounce reading the Bible to find arguments to justify our behavior or that of our group. Any time we read the Bible to find arguments or justifications, we wallow in Christian ideology.

If I read the Bible in order to listen to the questions God asks me about my thoughts, my behavior, my church, then I am well on the way to destroying ideology. This is because the first step toward criticizing ideologies as a group is to question Christian ideology. On that basis we can develop the possibility of an overall and radical challenge, which involves nonconformity to the world. The second step is understanding and applying Paul's teaching: "Do not be conformed to this world but be transformed by the renewal of your mind" (Rom. 12:2). This is typical of anti-ideological action. It involves discerning the sociological trends in our society. Precisely because they are sociological, they tempt us to join in with everyone else and, of course, to justify our actions ideologically. This rationalization appears to be a new understanding of the world, a belief in Progress, the Good, Justice, or Truth.

The touchstone in this case is to detect the sociological nature of the trend. "A given way of doing things appealed to no one twenty years ago; I would not have thought twice about it. Now it becomes fascinating, and I find it attractive. Why am I attracted? Because this thing is true, just, or good? No, since in that case I would have been interested twenty years ago. I find it tempting because the media give it attention and because so many millions follow and believe it."

Nudist behavior, for example, was not really "forbidden or suppressed" half a century ago; it simply did not exist, and nobody thought about it or *felt a need for it*. Today thousands of people find they have a frantic need to practice nudism. They feel scandalized when nudity is "suppressed," and consider nudism a conquest for freedom. But, of course, nudism exists as a need *only* because hundreds of thousands of people practice it and because we are given a rationalizing ideology of nudism. This means that there is no conquest for freedom involved, just obedience to a sociological trend. This is only one example.

Thus we detect purely ideological talk as the product of a trend involving many people who justify their behavior by such talk. Their behavior expresses only a major societal tendency. In other words, conforming to the "world" is evil compared with freedom in Christ, and we must fight such conformity's translation into ideology. I must detect how each ideology expresses conformity to society and attracts me. This process is doubly important since ideology involves me inevitably in false problems without importance.

We can look at this falsity in two ways. (1) As we have said, ideology is the degeneration of a doctrine. Such a doctrine was generally conceived as related to the reality its author lived in and the problems posed by that reality. But when, after a time, this doctrine was slowly popularized, made commonplace, and mixed with beliefs and passions, it ceased to refer to a genuine reality. Reality was left behind. For example, Marx's thought was worked out in relation to the problems of his time, with which he was admirably well acquainted. He offered precise solutions for these problems. But a century later, Marxist ideology continues to repeat a whole batch of formulas that no longer have any connection with the real problems of our time.

(2) In order to have an ideology large numbers of people must identify with it. I will not go into the problem of the amount of time lapsed: to succeed in having a large number of adherents, one must have time, so that when they have been gathered, they are mesmerized by problems that were *formerly true*, but *presently nonexistent*. Quite apart from this problem of time, large numbers of people will support an ideology only if it signifies conformity. They will follow an ideology that expresses what everybody believes and not something that raises questions. Heroes and saints can accept being called into question, but no one else can. Ideology spreads precisely to the degree that it changes nothing. Nazi ideology formulated and crystallized what millions of Germans already believed and wanted; it changed nothing essential.

Christianity attracts millions of followers (and becomes an ideology) when it begins to fill the religious void every person has within himself. This means that ideology concerns me with false problems, not really burning issues or dramatic, demanding matters. Ideology makes me think the moon is made of green cheese; that is, it impassions, dramatizing false problems, making me think they are important. The main significance of Christians' presence and of visible faith, then, is that they can denounce ideology and the false and outdated questions it raises.

Christians must discern the genuine issues of our time. This way we perform a genuine service to politics and to the society in which we live. We can do this by means of the discernment of spirits, but such understanding must be applied by means of a solid, rigorous, independent analysis of the political, economic, and sociological spheres. This sort of analysis is a practical matter, whereas the discernment of spirits makes it possible, safeguards it, and oversees it. Such analysis must be achieved based on a "point of view" different from that of all ideologies.

Even when they claim to be utopian, ideologies refer to a past reality, whereas our discernment is based on the certainty that Christ is coming, the certainty of the Kingdom as both already present and still to come. In other words the discernment of the true, concrete, political, and social problems of our present world is possible only starting from a vision of the Kingdom of God that is coming. This is true prophecy: the simple understanding of the present as it relates to the permanent truth of God. Certainly the Christian must be a prophet in our time; and prophecy is the exact opposite of all ideology.

2. Challenge

Before undertaking a critical analysis of the remarkable phenomenon of Marxist Christians, we must consider the positive aspect of the situation. Many Christians, over the past thirty years, have felt challenged by Marxism and Communism. Many have had a bad conscience because of what the searching gaze of socialism revealed about them, their church, or even Christianity itself. What were the grounds of this challenge?

First, it was obviously based on justice. In every respect our society is unjust for both individuals and groups. It produces inequality on all levels: inequality of opportunity, income, power, culture, etc. Indeed, society multiplies injustice. This unjust society results from twenty centuries of Christianity. And neither churches nor Christians are doing anything to improve the situation, to bring about justice. Over against this situation, Communism has as its objective the creation of a just society. We must understand this challenge.

The second basis of Communism's challenge that seems important to me springs from the first: the significance of poverty and the poor. On all levels and in every aspect of our society, the poor are rejected, mistreated, and forced more deeply into their poverty. Christianity should have taken up the cause of the poor; better yet, it should have identified with the poor. Instead, during almost the entire course of its history, the Church has served as a prop of the powerful and has been on the side of exploiters and states. The Church is numbered among the "powers"; it has sanctified the situation of the poverty-stricken. It provided theological justification for political regimes and tried to persuade the poor to accept their oppressed condition, all the while legitimizing their exploitation. The Church has truly functioned as the opium of the people. By so doing, it not only participated in the evil done to people, but above all it betrayed the teaching and the very person of Jesus.

Over against this position, however, Communism sides with the poor. It enters their struggle; in fact, that is all it does. No matter what kind of poverty the poor suffer, the Communists are on their side, and Communists alone are with them. Consequently, they accomplish what Christianity preaches but fails to practice.

This leads us to a third aspect of Communism's challenge to the Church. The resounding clash between words and deeds or life, as seen in churches and in the life of individual Christians, has become glaring and painful. We teach love of our neighbor and we exploit him; we preach about justice and produce injustice, etc. We said above that the world we have ended up with is the opposite of what Christ proclaimed, and the fault lies with Christianity. With the Communists, however, we find a completely different model: they practice what they preach. They achieve coherence between thought and action, theory and praxis. Let us not get tangled up in considerations of so-called Communist societies and the degree to which they practice Communism. The current response is well known: "But these countries (especially the Soviet Union) are not and have never been Communist." Well and good.

In spite of this consideration, there is consistency: not between the "ideal" (hardly a Communist term!) of justice and liberty that Communists proclaim and the applications of Stalinism, but between Lenin's analysis of strategy and tactics, for example, and what was accomplished. If you take seriously what Marx, and later Lenin, wrote concerning *tactics*, you see that its applications in the Soviet Union and in Prague, the violation of rights in Poland in 1947, etc.—all these are perfectly consistent with their writings. At this level there exists a consistency that attracts Christians, just as, on the intellectual level, there exists an admirably satisfactory harmony in the dialectical relationship between theory and practice.

The fourth aspect of Communism's challenge to the Church is "materialism." Christianity has progressively become a kind of disembodied spiritualism. Faith has become an individual and private matter, having to do with religious emotion, the inner life, feelings, and intentions, and sterile contemplation never translated into actions. Christians "feel" their faith rather than live it. We all recognize the easily criticized, yet genuine, dichotomy between the Sunday Christian and the same person as he lives during the rest of the week.

Such a life negates both the Old Testament and the incarnation of Jesus Christ. The Old Testament is utterly "materialist"; God enters the concrete life of His people and does not withdraw them from the world. He participates in history. The entire Old Testament is political history and not at all religious. It exalts the body, love in its carnal reality (the Song of Solomon!), and shows that nothing is experienced without the body. There exists no separation between a soul one could consider important and a body looked on as vile and lowly. The same is true of Paul's writings, in which the original meaning of "flesh" has been reestablished: it does not mean "body." The Old Testament probably fails to speak of an afterlife or an individual resurrection; certainly it knows no immortal soul or paradise![1]

As for Jesus, a simple reminder of His incarnation betrays the dreadful error involved in a disembodied Christianity. One can also see in the Gospels the importance of daily life, the body, and the undivided unity of being. Thus Christianity has utterly betrayed the very essence of revelation by transforming it into religious spirituality. Christianity has perverted Christian action by reducing it to a matter of individual conversion.

Marxism rubs our nose in this betrayal. It reminds us of the decisive importance of concrete, human life before death, and of the body and daily activity. But it also reminds us of the material quality of the sacrament: "This is my body." Marxism gives the impression of rehabilitating what Christianity has obscured. In accordance with the biblical message, Marxism drives Christianity into a corner: will we live it or not?

Marxism reveals the lie of this stripped-down evangelism, showing that if we have taken refuge in spiritual matters, we did so knowingly. We were not concerned with purity, for example, but with hiding what Christians really practiced. We wanted to be oriented toward heaven, so as not to see the injustice, poverty, and exploitation on earth. Communism has grasped everything Christians should have grasped. This "materialism" contains a basic recall of the very truth of the Bible. Materialism restores some weight to our flimsy spirituality.

Thus Christians must listen to this message, which also coincides with the rediscovery of history. Theologians have learned all over again that the God of Israel is a God of history, and that the whole Bible is a book of history rather than philosophy (or, even worse, metaphysics). But Christians had completely forgotten that the Bible relates events, not reasoning; they had become immersed in metaphysics.

We owe to Marx the rediscovery of this central truth (according to the popular understanding; actually Hegel preceded Marx on the issue of history and the Bible as history). Marx

---

1. At least this is true if we do not include the book of Wisdom (also known as the Wisdom of Solomon) in the canon, as the Catholic Church does.

brought history back to the light: not the history of historians, but history as we find it in the Bible: history filled with meaning, moving in a revealed direction, and culminating in an "apotheosis," but with everything "situated" in history. Here again Marx brings Christians back to revealed truth.

Finally, we must add a militant and communal spirit to the other ways in which Communism challenges the Church. Christians used to be, and should be, militant. And they have been called to make up a living, active community based on fraternity. But what do we see? Flabby, lazy, individualistic church members, committed to nothing. They sit beside each other on Sunday and proceed to ignore each other completely. They are capable of no sacrifice, they create nothing new. Whereas among Communists we find a militant spirit, commitment, a willingness to struggle and sacrifice, a community. How could Christians not be disturbed by this example and attracted by this carrying out of what the "Church" is proclaimed to be—and what they are not?

Christians have found all their discoveries in Marxism and Communism challenging. Such challenges are, of course, a severe trial for the Christian's bad conscience. One could respond by saying that, after all, Marx and Communists have nothing new to teach us. They have invented nothing, they say nothing the Christian did not already know. But in any case they represent a definite rediscovery. On the basis of their challenge, we can no longer escape the challenge of the Bible and of revelation itself!

Marxism and Communism represent an inevitable provocation. But their challenge also obliges us to recognize a remarkable convergence. The bourgeois church, with its spiritualism and traditionalism, contaminated by money and the powers, has tried to convince us that Marxism and Christianity stand in opposition to each other. But instead we find agreement, on two different levels. Recognizing this challenge moves us to take the next step: to take Christianity seriously again, to desire at last to be authentically Christian. Thus we were, to a great extent, encouraged to come to ourselves.

But will churches and Christianity be able to carry out the Bible's implications, this rediscovery of the meaning and value

of the revelation lived out in history? It is all very fine to rediscover the Bible's meaning, but living it out, fulfilling its message
in daily practice, is the important thing! Many Christians have
convinced themselves that the Church, Christian circles, and
Christianity were unreformable—that they would never carry
out their commitment in history. This commitment involves not
enabling people to become "Christians" so much as enabling
them to become simply human! It involves bringing about the
minimum of justice required by Scripture, so that a poor person
could again represent Christ to us. If the Church fails to accomplish this task, who will do it? Now we have the answer: Communism will do it.

Thus we move beyond the stage of listening to a challenge
to noting an agreement, and from this observation we move on
to seeing conformity at the level of action. Christians find they
are no longer called just to become more Christlike, but they
believe that in order to become better Christians, they must
cooperate with the Communists. They feel they must adopt a
practice for which Communism holds the secret. Christians
must make history with them, since history belongs to the poor.

From that point, it is easy to see how Christians come to the
conclusion that they must prove that theology should be materialistic, that the Bible must be read in a new manner, etc. In
other words, they come to a new interpretation of Christianity
based on the discovery that they have a political practice in common with Communism. This is, I believe, more or less the way
thinking has moved these past thirty years.

Now, however, we must see what lies behind this thinking.
I want to declare that by exploring this issue, I show that I am
just as good a Marxist as the others. After all, Marx himself
teaches us on the one hand not to leave anything unclarified,
and on the other to look beyond appearances and superficial
talk. Thus can we discover the hidden, anonymous sociological
process at work where the speaker claims that he takes his position only because of his conviction and on the basis of the truth
that has finally come to light.

Chapter II

Christians and Socialism: Conformity*

1. Origins of Marxist Christianity

In Christian circles[1] we find ourselves witnessing a second flood of theses, books, manifestos, and movements concerned with Christianity and Marxism, or, more accurately, Christians and socialism: "socialist Christians, materialist (i.e., Marxist) approaches to the gospel, Christian campaigns for Marxist parties, declarations of 'Marxist-Christian doctrine,'" etc. The Left would not win in either Italy or France without the considerable contribution of the Christian electorate, which is determined by ideology rather than by social class.

All this activity is reminiscent of a similar outpouring of effort in France in 1944, when Christians had discovered the companionship of Communists in the Resistance. On the basis of this common effort Christians felt attracted to the socialist struggle for justice and peace. Then we saw Father Montuclard's Progressive Christians, the Partisans of Peace, the Movement for Peace, etc. We must remember what these fine people supported with all their fervor: Joseph Stalin and Stalinism, nothing else. They were fiercely hostile to any mention of the Stalinist dictatorship or the concentration camps, which were known to exist. These Christians bear a heavy responsibility for the existence of the Gulag, which they energetically defended.

---

* Most of the material in this chapter was previously published, with minor differences, as "Les Crétiens et le Socialisme," *Contrepoint*, no. 25 (1978), 37-50.—TRANS.

1. Obviously, my analysis deals with Christians in non-Communist countries. Nothing in this book attacks such remarkable and relevant undertakings as Igor Orgoutsov's Christian Social Union in the Soviet Union.

But our problem today is different. Christian Communists were blind back in 1944, but their children's parallel blindness today has taken a different direction.

Christians are, as usual, several steps behind, because they think they are following the latest progressive thought when they subscribe piously to the predominant ideological trend. Christians wait to get stirred up about Marx's thought and the movements it inspired until the best Marxist thinkers have either completely abandoned Communism (and sometimes Marx's thought as well), or have concluded that we must radically revise what Marx wrote. Many Marxist intellectuals, including H. Lefebvre, E. Morin (both of whom took a critical stance long ago), D. Desanti, C. Castoriadis, P. Daix, C. Lefort, and A. Glucksman, came to the conclusion that they had been utterly mistaken.

These intellectuals' eminently honest and critical undertaking entailed two basic questions: (1) "How could we have been blind for so long? How could we have done such fuzzy thinking during the entire Stalinist era; mustn't we be on our guard now, as a result?" (2) "Stalin cannot have been a historical accident. He was surely the consequence of Lenin, and perhaps even the result of Marx. Can it be that, by some chance, Marxism inevitably produces Stalinist Communism? We must reread Marx in the light of the Gulag." And since the responses of L. Althusser and J. Ellenstein, since Jean Kanapa's death, the only remaining intellectual who maintains at all costs his unwavering faithfulness to Marx and the Communist Party is Pierre Juquin. That is not much.

Now, then, we see Christians coming to the rescue! They no longer bother with the matter of doctrine: the compatibility of Marx's materialism with the affirmation of a transcendent God, earlier considered the central problem, these Christians view as utterly obsolete. It seems childish, flowing from an outmoded idealist philosophy.

We must consider this attitude carefully, however; it implies that we have already passed *beyond* the problem. That is, after a person has subscribed to materialist philosophy, he can then declare this problem of materialism versus a transcendent God to be superseded. Of course, one makes this declaration without having resolved the difficulty: one simply dismisses it, as Marx effectively did. Such a brushing aside presupposes an irrational and fideistic adherence to materialist philosophy.

Even more importantly, by ignoring the conflict between a transcendent God and a materialist philosophy, Christians also fail to address a practical matter: until now, without exception, in every country where it has been applied, Marxism has given birth to the worst sort of dictatorships, to strictly totalitarian regimes (including China and Vietnam). This matter is not even recalled. In other words, Marxist Christians analyze neither the theoretical problem of Marxism's compatibility with Christianity nor the problem of its practice. What do they consider, then? Their basic concern is to reinterpret Christianity by means of Marxism, and to transpose their action onto the terrain demarcated by Communism. This concern keeps them so occupied they have no time to examine the context and the upshot of the problem! In other words, they have already entered *within* Marxist-Communist ideology; they have crossed over the line into the movement without examining their decision. They subscribe to the cause on the basis of its obvious justice, and in so doing they have taken a considerably greater step than the Christians who approached Communists in 1944.

Such Christians in our day have failed to realize that they conform to the unfortunately traditional Christian habit of always looking for a way to adapt Christianity to the dominant intellectual and sociological trend. The current commitment of Christians to "socialism-Marxism-Communism"[2] testifies to what a degree this tendency has become the dominant ideology in our society.

Christians have *always* functioned in the same way: in a given society, a dissenting ideology comes on the scene. Christians fail to observe it. If the ideology grows, they begin to find it interesting, but they refrain from getting involved. If it becomes the dominant ideology (in which case it continues to dissent from the established reality!), the traditional ideology begins to decline seriously. At this point, when the dissenting

---

2. For obvious reasons I make no attempt to define these three terms. The stance of Christians is so nebulous that all three have to be combined to describe their position.

ideology is certain to win out, Christians rush to get on the
bandwagon, thus becoming "extremists." These neophytes, full
of courage and radicalism, try to demonstrate their extremism.
But in reality, such "extremism" is nothing but a slavish following of the current sociological trend, often just when this ideology, having become dominant, enters its own crisis of decline.
A certain number of Christians, of course, remain faithfully
wedded to yesterday's ideology, or even to the one that
preceded it. In this case, the Church becomes a battleground
where conservatives struggle against progressives.

All of this demonstrates that Christians are utterly unable to
express revelation in a way that is both specific and adequate
for the social reality in which they live. They either repeat timeless formulas (which they take to be eternal), or else they initi-
ate a pseudo-rereading of the Bible: in reality a method of har-
monizing biblical content with the dominant ideology. In this
way Christians constitute an important contributing
sociopolitical force on the side of the tendency which is about to
dominate. As a result, they obtain a small place in the new social order.

This pattern has repeated itself over and over for the last
1500 years, every time social upheaval has taken place. And
Constantinianism is not the explanation for it! As soon as a social model appears as "Truth" to the great majority (always a
diffuse, nebulous truth, of course), Christians subscribe to it,
whether it is the King or the Republic, Magianism or Rational-
ity, Scientism or Religion, Power or Anti-Power (for we must remember all the mass movements hostile to politically established power!). Original, specific inventions in the area of
Christian thought and conduct have been extremely rare. They
have usually been temporary and overshadowed by collective
support of the latest ideology. The present Marxist-Christian
tendency is simply another wrinkle in the consistent Christian
attitude throughout history.

We must, however, examine the most debatable aspect of
this analysis: has Marxism become the dominant ideology in
our society? This thought poses serious problems, in particular:
how could such a thing happen, in view of the dogma that the
prevailing ideology comes from the ruling class? How can we

explain socialist ideology being spread by the universities, for instance, since they belong to what has been called (since Althusser) the "ideological apparatus of the State"? This expression is spouted by all the "neos" as if it were new and explained something!

At this point we must demonstrate two things: (1) that Marxism has lost all content and specificity, that it has thus become an ideology in the worst sense (and is no longer a theory or even a doctrine); (2) that the vague, remaining Marxism is the overall atmosphere we all share.

What is left of Marx in our day? Nothing. I say "nothing" even though I take Marxists themselves into account. What do they think of Marx's political economy? It has been quietly swept into a corner; it contains so many errors, ill-conceived explanations, and false predictions that Marxists generally prefer not to mention Marx's political economy in concrete terms. What about Marx's philosophy? Insofar as it attempted to provide a coherent materialist system, Marxists have usually abandoned it as well, so that materialism is no longer considered an essential axiom. Marx's materialism was necessarily tied to the overall thought of the nineteenth century. And Marx's strategy? Why, Communism was supposed to come to life in the most economically developed country, where capitalism had reached its greatest potential. There is no need for us to labor this point: the debate on this issue has been well known since the conflict between K. Kautsky and Lenin. In our day we have changed all this: now Communism can come to life in the most poverty-stricken countries. But this is profoundly anti-Marxist; even the most convoluted explanation fails to harmonize the two notions.

What remains, then, are scattered pieces of Marx's thought; Marxists clutch at these, as if by themselves they could have some obscure meaning: class struggle, prevailing ideology, relations of production, etc. Certain quotations of Marx are especially useful—profound phrases that get applied to everything, and that can be interpreted however one likes! As a result, some people marvel: how miraculous that after the end of Stalinism, there are dozens of Marxisms to choose from! Althusser's is unlike Daix's; A. Gramsci surfaces, but differs from Mao. You have a whole gamut of Marxisms to choose from, depending on your size, your ideas, and your place in society. Wonderful how our freedom has progressed! Unfortunately, Marx's thought is utterly gutted as a result: it lies lifeless and incoherent.

Communism also empties itself of its previously essential tenets. This discovery matters as much as the points we have already examined. The French Communist Party has abandoned the dictatorship of the proletariat. This could amount to a simple tactical declaration (we must remember that the dictatorship of the proletariat was previously solemnly abandoned in Poland in 1946 and in Czechoslovakia in 1947). If not, it is a colossal revision of everything the Communist Party has always taught. Can Communism be established without such a dictatorship? Until now there had never been any doubt: such a thing was viewed as impossible. The French Communist Party's suggested substitute for the doctrine of the dictatorship of the proletariat is so vague and inconsistent that it fails utterly to satisfy. Furthermore, if you uphold the proposition of class struggle, how can you avoid affirming the dictatorship of the proletariat? Nobody seems to ask this question. Such inconsistency is all too common when people move to the most superficial ideological level.

Internationalism was another basic tenet of Communism. Now we witness the appearance of national Communisms. This does not involve the old argument concerning whether Communism is possible in a single country; rather we are observing the actual appearance of a different Communism in each nation, taking on national characteristics. Furthermore, these Communisms are nationalistic; that is, instead of proclaiming that the nation is evil and a bourgeois entity to be destroyed, now we hear that we must defend our national sovereignty and independence and prepare for war against anyone who might try to attack us. What an astonishing about-face!

Impoverishment has met the same fate: after a last stand on the issue in 1954, Marxists finally recognized that no pauperization affects workers, and that Marx's famous law to the contrary does not exist. In this connection the potentially revolutionary class has been almost indefinitely extended. Since the working class is no longer unified or poverty-stricken (for the most part), Marxists have extended the concept of the proletariat to include all salaried workers. Terminology shifted from the term *proletariat*, which now serves only for certain speeches and proclamations, to the *salaried worker*. Whatever your status, standard of living, or function in society, if you receive a salary, you belong to the proletariat, because of the magical "relationship with respect to the means of production as private property." This broader definition of the proletariat amounts to another amazing retraction, since it involves abandoning the vocation to defend and gather together the exploited and alienated!

We can conclude this brief review by admiring how values have been reintroduced within Communism. Marx vituperated continually against values such as justice, liberty, equality, etc., but the Communist Party has become the biggest consumer of values. It constantly presents itself as the defender of these magic words, which it carefully refrains from defining, and which allow, amazingly enough, for the reintegration of democracy within Communism. Astounded, we observe how the Communist Party today proclaims exactly the opposite of the traditional Marxist-Communist affirmation concerning juridical freedoms and bourgeois democracy. Juridical freedoms such as the right to vote were previously considered not only worthless (so that they could be abolished with no problem) but also pernicious and utterly negative, because they tricked the proletariat and prevented it from revolting. Thus it was necessary to combat such freedoms with determination. Well, that has all changed now! Communists must carefully defend, and even extend, juridical freedoms, loyally playing along with liberal, constitutional, parliamentary democracy, since democracy is considered the best road to socialism.

In summary, we have witnessed in recent years the rejection of *everything* that made the Communist Party hard and uncompromising. All rough edges and areas of disagreement with other political orientations have been eliminated, along with all of Communism's key affirmations. Could this change amount to a mere tactic? I do not think so; I believe that Communism (in general and in all its forms) is so thoroughly spread and integrated into our society, so utterly assimilated to our present world, and so completely penetrated by the various prevailing ideologies that it has lost all its vigor and specificity. The result is a kind of ideological stew into which you can throw anything, so long as it agrees with the ideology of the clientele.

This clientele has expanded enormously. It no longer brings with it a hard and pure concept of the most die-hard socialism. Instead, it is subject to the most ordinary stream of beliefs, desires, needs, and tendencies. These Communists are not the militants of old, but supporters who are also voters. Thus the influence goes two ways: the Communist Party abandons the most essential tenets of its doctrine so as to attract a wider clientele, but this clientele brings with it a body of ideas and feelings utterly contrary to what Communism has always stood for. These new supporters are nationalists who believe in democracy, freedom, equality, etc., and their goals are comfort, happiness, and a higher standard of living. Obviously, since Marxism and Communism have been utterly voided of content, people can join up with no difficulty.

Across from my house stands a wonderful billboard: "These days it is *natural* to join the French Communist Party!" Of course! Fifty years ago, there was nothing *natural* about it: it was a heroic decision implying commitment to abnegation and continual conflict in the most difficult of paths. Now this act becomes natural, since the party no longer requires any intellectual conversion. Communism's complete about-face enables anyone to join up with ease.

We can say, then, that present-day Communism has become an ideology in the most vulgar sense of the word. It is worthless: a bunch of beliefs, a mixture of all sorts of things, since it has grasped everything that belonged to our society's mood. Communism is the most perfected ideology, because it makes use of absolutely everything that makes up the ideological panorama of our society. It expresses our state of mind and has spread everywhere, because it has given the label "Communist" to the various feelings-beliefs-commonplaces-ideas that are present everywhere. Communism has taken the lowest common denominator of all French people and adopted this as its doctrine. As a result, nothing prevents the average French person any longer from joining that which calls itself Communism, and then he can become a member of the organization representing this Communism: the French Communist

Party. In so doing, a person simply moves from the vague state of mind in which he lives naturally to becoming formally a member of the organization that best typifies that state of mind.

This matter of influence is a two-way street. The French Communist Party has adopted previously existing beliefs, but certain traditionally Marxist and Communist ideas have also spread throughout society, so that even people on the Right believe them automatically, without critical reflection. Here are a few examples of Marxist axioms that have spread and now belong to everyone's thinking: the economic explanation of social phenomena; de facto materialism; generalized historicism; the elimination of the Subject; liberation from moral taboos; questioning the predominant morality; and applying "dialectics" to absolutely everything.

Curiously, these attitudes have become the common ground of our society because they belonged to the bourgeoisie's *previous* ideology. The bourgeoisie has always been materialistic, so that as soon as the strict, die-hard dialectical materialism of Marx was eliminated, agreement was easily reached. The same holds true for the economic explanation of social phenomena: the bourgeoisie as a class, long before Marx, explained everything on economic grounds, but hid this under a veil of idealism. Now that the Communist Party has taken the veil of the same idealism and abandoned rigorous economic explanations, agreement and the spread of this idea are easily accomplished.

Thus, on these different grounds, we realize that Communism has become a pure ideology—the prevailing one. We live in this climate, feed on these ideas daily, whatever our opinions may be. The only possible problem is the word *Communist;* we balk at the name "French Communist Party." But if it were called, for example, the "Guaranteed Democracy Party," there would no longer be anything standing in the way of 99% of French citizens' joining it.

We need to go further, however. Communist ideology dominates because it has become the ideology of common consumption, but also for three other reasons. (1) Communism remains the only potentially overall explanation of history, of economic

evolution, and of certain concrete developments (unemploy-
ment, inflation, etc.). And we can never live without an overall
explanation for things. We have an absolute need for a complete
frame of reference: a satisfying system that allows us to understand what we are experiencing. All other overall explanations
(Christianity in particular) have disappeared. With its traditional explanatory system now blended with all the ideological
contributions we have examined, Communism offers the
(purely fictitious and illusory) possibility of understanding. It
apparently allows people to understand and explain what is
happening in their world, as filtered through the media.

Communism is wonderfully Manichean, enabling a person
to identify clearly good and evil, to distinguish the good guys
from the bad guys; it also shows what one must do so that good
may triumph. Under these circumstances, it is no wonder that
Communism has become the frame of reference to which people
cling, so as not to feel lost in a crazy world.

The two other essential new factors I will merely mention
here, referring the reader to my earlier published studies on the
subject. (2) On the one hand, Communism has become our
society's greatest provider of commonplaces. It stands as the
Bouvard et Pécuchet[3] of 1970. Everyone recognizes what he has
always believed in the "truths" dispensed by the revolutionary
medium.[4]

(3) On the other hand, the ruling class also participates in
this frenzied clinging to Communist ideology: film directors,
artists, capitalists, professors, high-level executives—little by
little they join the crowd. In this connection I believe we must
keep in mind a remarkable phenomenon that takes place at
times in history: the death wish of a society's ruling classes—a
drive toward suicide. The nobility at the time of the French Revolution provide us with an example. They cling, with revulsion
and irresistible attraction, to their death-dealing beliefs. The
Parisian salons are another case in point.[5] Although I accept that

---

3. Gustave Flaubert, 1881.—TRANS.

4. On this point, see my *A Critique of the New Commonplaces*, trans.
Helen Weaver (New York: Knopf, 1968).

5. See my *Métamorphose du bourgeois* (Paris: Calmann-Lévy, 1967).

the prevailing ideas are those of the ruling classes, at times this class, obsessed with suicide, promotes the very prevailing ideology most contrary to its interests. This ideology will condemn the ruling class to death. Thus, up to a certain point, the ruling classes are the agents who congeal this widespread collective ideology into the prevailing ideology. But they follow neither their own interests nor their desire for domination: they are motivated by their death wish.

French Communist Party strategy has understood perfectly all this basic yet complex development. Fortunately the so-called "Marxist" justification for this development has been exposed. Thanks to the theory of the "historical block" (a somewhat twisted version of Gramsci's concept!), it has become perfectly possible to participate in the revolutionary movement without necessarily belonging to the proletariat. As a corollary, thanks to the new interpretation of mutual influences between the superstructure and the infrastructure, the relative independence of the elements of the superstructure, overdetermination, etc., a person may become a Communist on purely ideological and revolutionary grounds—even if he belongs objectively to the ruling classes. Doctrinal purity is safeguarded.

In reality, however, the present tendency to identify with the Left (particularly with Communism) is strictly a matter of going with the stream, being carried along by the wind. Such adhesion is a purely sociological matter, without value or significance. The person who declares himself a Communist today is the same one who would have been a French Nationalist in 1914, a Monarchist in 1830, a follower of Napoleon in 1804, etc.

This being the case, when Christians undertake impressive-sounding research on the subject, it amounts to mere pieces of paper "tossed by every wind of doctrine." In view of the gutting of Communism's content, clearly no obstacle remains to a Christian's joining up. By becoming Communists, Christians follow the general trend and need feel no pricks of conscience or theological reservations. They conform culturally and intellectually to the rest of society. They already represented the prevailing ideology of the "ruling classes," and by joining Communism, they simply reinforce this trend.

In this movement, however, Christianity is of course also

gutted of all content. This process is facilitated by the pseudo-scientific affirmation that everything is cultural. Since the entire content of God's revelation in Jesus Christ is cultural anyway, one need have no compunctions about getting rid of the outmoded past. What is left of the revelation? Obviously, since the Christian has joined up with Communism, the defender of the poor and the voice of the oppressed, Christianity becomes (in its entirety) the defense of the poor. This includes armed defense, political struggle, etc.

This description is by no means hypothetical; rather, it is precisely what I have observed in a large number of Christians. Their thinking does not begin with the content of revelation in favor of the poor and oppressed. Instead, (1) they are profoundly (and genuinely—I do not suspect their motives) moved by the wretchedness of this world's poor; (2) they are tempted by socialism; (3) they find socialism's worldview satisfying and its means appropriate for the struggle; (4) they become Communists; and then (5) they mold their interpretation of Christianity to harmonize with their decision. These are the five stages I have repeatedly seen people go through. And these neo-Marxist Christians, with their fundamental honesty, their militant spirit, and the zeal of the newly converted, will shortly become utterly uncompromising and will aim for the most rigorous possible doctrine. They will take their place on the extreme edge of the movement they joined, unknowingly through sociological conformism.

Furthermore, we cannot avoid recognizing the role of terrorism and fascination in Communism's attraction for Christians. Today Marxism is the only terrorist line of thought in Western intellectual circles. It claims to be the only scientific thought, systematically destroying all other approaches. It professes to be a complete explanation without gaps. It holds all phenomena in subordination. By Marxist methods, of course, it also explains Christian faith, along with Jesus' preaching, the writing of the books of the Bible, and the development of the Church. Marxism explains everything and encloses everything within its methods, which claim to be more vast and all-encompassing than Christianity.

Marxism also excludes Christianity through "reduction":

Christianity cannot make any claim to truth or uniqueness; it is just one of many subordinate phenomena, from the point of view of Marxism. Marxist doctrine requires confrontation, and its inroads are such that one can no longer claim to do any thinking unless he takes a position with respect to Marxism.

Marxist totalitarian thinking, which is both inclusive and exclusive, is not only a form of thought, however. It rests on an administrative, organizational, and political structure that amounts to a genuine machine—a war machine, designed for the conquest of power and the subversion of society. This machine has no pity; it is totalitarian and harsh as it practices both inward terrorism (purges and self-criticism) and outward terrorism (threats directed against the enemy, who will inevitably be overcome and eliminated). These two kinds of terrorism reinforce each other.

Remarkably enough, Communism manages, in Euro-Communism, etc., to appear benevolent, full of understanding, to have a human face (and what face has ever been more paternal and human than Stalin's?—he seemed a veritable benevolent god). Meanwhile, the effects of terrorism continue, and this human face is clearly just a paternal image covering up Communism as a whole. Underneath, the appearance of discipline never lets up, nor does the determination to acquire exclusive power. Correlatively, intellectual terrorism did not disappear along with Stalinism; on the contrary! Precisely when Marxist thought ceases to be reduced to a catechism it becomes fully terrorist. "Come now, you must have bad intentions and be a poor intellectual if you do not see that everything has its place and is explained by our dialectic. There is nothing authoritarian or simplistic about it. Take G. Lukacs, or consider Gramsci or Althusser; notice their diversity, how broad and conscientious they are. . . ." But their work is supported by the most powerful party, the greatest army, and the imperialist force that has conquered the most; half the world's population expresses allegiance to this doctrine. "Supported?" No, of course, not directly. No one aims a gun at your head. But how can we neglect these little matters when speaking of Marxism and Communism? How could we possibly forget them? How could they fail to occupy our subconscious? And along with them, we have the Gulag, which officials of course rejected and condemned. But its presence is still with us, because it could always return.

Who can guarantee that this Communism, which seems so paternal today, will not go back to being the Communism of the Gulag and of the Loubianka when it comes to power tomorrow? Leninism itself warns us that this must happen. You reject Lenin? But Lenin himself recommends terrorism in order to consolidate power. We cannot disassociate the concrete terrorism of Marxist thought from the political terrorism of Stalinism as it remains engraved on our subconscious.

In the specific domain of the French intellectual world, moreover, you can be taken seriously only if you take a position within or with respect to Marxism. Obviously you are uninteresting and none of your ideas has any weight or meaning unless you participate in one of the current exercises: new interpretation of Marx; application of Marx's method to new areas; analysis of political phenomena by means of latent Marxism; opposition to Stalinism in the name of Marx; reinterpretation of forgotten texts; discovery of the Marxism contrary to Marx; an ex-Stalinist explains his repentance; conversions from Marxism to Christianity; attempt to synthesize everything in Marxist thought, etc.

The terrorist position consists of situating everything with respect to Marxism. Marxism dominates in this way not because of Marxism's concrete importance, but because of the intellectual milieu's estimation of Marxism. Most amazing of all, this terrorist position became entrenched just as Marxism officially renounced its dogmatism and exclusivity. All the intellectuals who still had reservations, who could not bring themselves to accept Marxism's dogmatism and doctrinal authoritarianism, melted at the sight of this open Marxist thought, this Communism with a human face. Now everyone could join in with no qualms or remorse, since humanism and Marxism had at last been reconciled.

In this way the influence of Marxist thought grew *just when experienced Marxists ceased believing it*. This influence had been well prepared, certainly, by a thirty-year invasion of Marxist concepts, patterns, and explanations. These were taken as axiomatic and applied uncritically in every direction. Marxist language asserted itself as a scientific certainty and as the precise reflection of the facts. Demonstration was superfluous. Marxism had become an established truth, recognized by everyone. Outside this vocabulary, nothing could be taken seriously, since all else remained inevitably influenced by idealism. Thus we have both at the same time: a doctrinal terrorism and, alongside, an unconscious group terrorism. But this group was no longer explicitly Communist; it was made up of ordinary intellectuals, professors, and literary figures who had adopted the Marxist style automatically.

Fascination complements terrorism. Terrorism exercises its influence not only through fear but also as part of the sacred. Terrorism is both the *tremendum* and the *fascinans*. In spite of the risk it poses, terrorism attracts everything around it, seducing and drawing into its orbit, provoking imitation. Once fascinated by terrorism, a person can no longer see any different reality, any other truth. He begins to use terrorist language and becomes a terrorist.

Western intellectuals have clustered in this way around Marxism since 1945; they do not become card-carrying Communists, but they can no longer tear themselves away from this fascination. They are held in its sway even when in a moment of lucidity they recognize its illusory quality (J.-P. Sartre being a typical case). They are held by Marxism's fascination because, apart from all the glamor and arguments, Marxism seems to offer the ultimate value: a scientific and all-encompassing explanation of our history, society, and world. And, in a shift we can easily understand, since Marxism *offers* an overall explanation, it must *be* the explanation.

Thus we cannot content ourselves with studying Marx in his time: his analysis of nineteenth-century capitalism, nineteenth-century class struggle, his retrospective view of history based on this position, the revolutionary interpretation that could be given in his time, etc. No, Marx's modern followers consider these matters as only the temporal expression of a universal system. Everything in the modern world *must* also be explained in the same manner (this "must," not explicitly stated, serves to undergird the entire intellectual movement and shows the role of hallucination and fascination in this mode of thinking). Marxism must also serve to explain things Marx never knew or even suspected.

Distressing gaps appear between what Marx clearly said and what he must be made to say if he is to continue providing a complete, unfailing explanation for absolutely everything. For instance, Marxist psychoanalysis needs developing. This example is significant but not at the simplistic level suggested by W. Reich: "We have Freud on the one hand and Marx on the other. How to reconcile them, to construct a 'Freudo-Marxism'? How can Freud [who objected to Marxism] be integrated into this method, and how can Communists be persuaded to accept psychoanalysis [when they mistrust it]?"

Reich's very elementary approach has been completely superseded. G. Deleuze and F. Guattari provide us with a much more significant model for our day: "Marxism? Unrelated to what we are saying! Doctrinal synthesis? Of course not!" Yet in spite of such denials, their writings involve a well-camouflaged latent Marxism. They propose an "analysis" (which is not "psycho") based on an unavowed Marxist construction. They interpret everything as a machine, in terms of production and economics (since capitalism is evil itself), based on class division, fascist paranoia, and schizophrenic revolutionaries. Finally, they indict the family, not as the cause of neuroses, but as nonexistent. Such essentially "Marxist" positions lead to a *different* analysis of the so-called mentally-ill person. In Deleuze and Guattari's writings, the reader or listener finds himself unconsciously within the Marxist circle of thought.

In exactly the same manner, Marxist-materialist theology develops. The fascinated individual takes Marxism for science, since it gives us true categories and effects the only valid analysis of our world, providing us with a unique tool for intellectual inquiry. Such a person sees no reason to avoid elaborating a theology on the basis of Marxism; it would provide us at last with a theology we can take seriously, since it would be scientific for the first time. "Why not do this?" he asks himself. And he hears everyone respond, "Yes, why not? Very interesting. Although we are not even vaguely Marxist, we must be broad-minded. Why should we reject such an experiment? Why not do a Marxist-materialist analysis of the Scriptures? As serious intellectuals, how can we neglect this opportunity to have a *different* theological point of view? We have to look at all points of view and make use of all the evidence."

This attitude betrays dilettantism rather than intellectual responsibility, since it finds everything fascinating. Kierkegaard placed such "seriousness" in his lowest category: "interesting"—the opposite of serious. After all, many other theological points of view might also be "interesting"—the devil's, for example! Those who develop Marxist-materialist theology are simply spellbound (we must remember that Marx did theology);[6] those who listen to such theologians and follow them are dilettantes. In our time, when Christians subscribe to a decaying, waning Marxism, such an attitude is quite appropriate.

2. A Case in Point

We will now examine several specific issues with reference to a work by R. Chapuis, who provides us with a startling testimony concerning the Christian approach to Marxism.[7] As a young traditional Catholic, born in a conservative blue-collar family, Chapuis belonged to the Catholic Youth Movement, prepared to enter the Ecole Normale Supérieure, and gradually became a Leftist Catholic, then a Christian Socialist, and finally a kind of socialist based on a reinterpretation of Christianity. In his book, a model of honesty, he indirectly and unintentionally reveals important matters. We can begin by analyzing the unrecognized presuppositions sprinkled throughout Chapuis's book, then his motives and development, ending with the "theoretical" debate he places at the conclusion.

First of all, Chapuis's presuppositions, of which he is unaware, have extraordinary significance.[8] I believe Chapuis

---

6. Marx produced neither a science nor a philosophy. His work was a genuine theology, with a transcendence, a soteriology, an eschatology, and an ethics. See my *The New Demons*, trans. C. Edward Hopkin (New York: Seabury; London: Mowbrays, 1975).

7. Robert Chapuis, *Les Chrétiens et le socialisme* (Paris: Calmann-Lévy, 1976). Chapuis's title is inaccurate: he deals rather with French Catholics and the socialist movement.

8. This brief analysis of uncritically assumed presuppositions, never

makes four uncritically assumed prejudgments, which he never states explicitly, and on which his whole argument rests:

(1) The essence of Christianity amounts to helping the poor. Love expresses itself exclusively in helping the poor person in such a way as to liberate him from the scourge of poverty. Apart from this, Christianity seems utterly empty. Faith, salvation, and the like are outmoded cultural forms that have served to oppress the poor. We all know the argument: Jesus became poor. Since we love Him, we must love the poor. The poor person represents all of Jesus. The poor person in himself is sufficient. Love means supporting him in his political struggle. Otherwise, saying we love (or pray, etc.) amounts to lying and hypocrisy.

(2) Socialism is identified with the human good. But Chapuis offers no details; he uses "socialism," a vague, many-faceted term, only in its overall sense. It represents the only path to our good.

(3) Communists are on the side of the poor and always defend them. In this connection as well, the author's vagueness is remarkable. Communism represents the road to a just and noble socialism. Chapuis says nothing about the problems of Communism. He mixes together the poor, the proletariat, and the workers. By definition, naturally, the Communist Party is the party of the poor.

(4) Action is all that matters. Furthermore, Chapuis considers action as principally, if not exclusively, political in nature. Any action not practical or concrete holds no interest. "Being a

---

explicitly expressed, seems to me essential if we are to understand and situate Chapuis's work. In the course of this book, I will return to this issue several times. The presuppositions of a text matter more, I believe, than what it says. They come to light when we ask the question, What basis does this statement or position have? After we have eliminated a certain number of secondary matters, we find ourselves left with a hard, irreducible kernel, which we soon recognize as unconscious in the author's thinking. Therefore he has not expressed, let alone criticized, these axioms and postulates that seem "evident" to him. Often we can detect presuppositions by looking for themes that should logically enter into the whole, but which the author never mentions or deals with methodically. He considers them "givens," and this fact reveals the true meaning of his work—much more so than the matters he affirms.

Christian means taking responsibility for this world's conflicts; it means carrying out an *action*" (the poor, stupid contemplatives believed that being a Christian meant adoring God through prayer). This thought continues in eloquent fashion: "*Therefore*, the Christian finds in Marxism the science of action he needs." We could observe that military and capitalist strategies are also sciences of action. But Chapuis would certainly not conclude that the Christian should become a capitalist or a general, since the presupposition of the primacy of action joins the three others.

At this point we must examine Chapuis's motives for moving from Catholicism to socialism. I believe two sorts of motives appear clearly, both expressions of the typical Catholic personality. The first: thirst for good works, particularly on the social plane. Faith takes a back seat with respect to works. Strangely, Catholics seem not to realize how their desire for commitment springs from their theology of good works. The desire for *social* and *political* commitment represents the ongoing tradition of the Catholic Church, which has always claimed to mold society's social and political structures. Chapuis is utterly traditional in this respect (except, of course, for the fact that the "mold" required now differs from the sixteenth-century one!).

Chapuis's second motive related to Catholicism: the debate with the hierarchy and the authoritarian structure of the institution. He shows clearly and concretely his move to radicalize his position so as to escape the hierarchy's effort to co-opt him. He adopts socialism in order to certify the independence of his commitment. Again, although this debate is typically Catholic, Chapuis appears not to recognize that the same attitude and reactions have occurred throughout the history of the Church. Nothing new is happening here: Catholicism has always included an enormous group antagonistic to its hierarchy and the institution. Such groups enable the institution to function better!

Finally, the Algerian war, with all the problems it posed for young people, formed the occasion for Chapuis's about-face. But he shows that these problems, when pushed to their limit, led him in the end to new positions in politics, metaphysics, and theology.

Now we must consider Chapuis's argument. Here again we find fascinating issues: Christianity and socialism, for example. A theoretical debate? A philosophical or theological question? By no means. What about Marxism? If cornered, Chapuis would answer "I do not know much about it." The only work of Marx's we can be sure he has read is the *Manifesto* (I cannot say whether he has read other works by Marx; he makes only this specific reference). In Chapuis's book we find no effort to understand what Marx's thought means for a Christian and the difficulties it involves. We find no application of Marxist "science." He reduces everything to what happened: how he became a Leftist, then a socialist, etc., because he had good pals who thought that way, with the same feelings, impressions, and emotions; they followed the same news programs. What we witness here is the illuminating formation of a milieu and a trend through mutual mimicry. Young people react directly to an event, influence each other, discover noble ideas, hate evil, long for a great hope, reject the fossilized past, and take their place in opposition to rules seen as too rigid. Thus we see how contact with chums who have already become Leftist produces Leftist convictions, without any understanding of what is involved.

Chapuis's book reflects this process admirably, with its swarms of people, committees, conferences, symposiums, militants, and intertwined threads. We witness the birth of a political stratum, as well as of a Leftist consciousness. The convictions born in this manner become reinforced, hardened, and radicalized through action and opposition. People join the Left because of sentimental adolescent idealism; then they become socialists, moving closer and closer to Communism, by means of their practical involvement. This move becomes easy when they are assured that Christianity is essentially action—just like Communism. Chapuis never raises the basic question of the possible contradictions between Marx's thought and the Bible. After all, those are just old hypocrites' objections!

At the end of Chapuis's book, however, we find an effort at theoretical formulation, which we will examine as we finish considering the matter of poverty. We must make two observations at this point. First, nothing can make a dent in the imperturbable certainty of our Leftist Catholic (who moves farther and farther to the Left). He fails to be troubled by the fact that many of his friends leave Christianity to become Communists. After all, he realizes that if he had to choose, he would opt for the struggle on the side of the oppressed. For Chapuis, being a Christian gradually loses any meaning except for political commitment. We will see, for example, the degree to which Jesus Christ disappears from this whole enterprise.

The same can be said of de-Stalinization. The Gulag? Really, now! A single line deals with the subject, to tell us that de-Stalinization is "monstrous." Nothing troubles Chapuis's convictions. Czechoslovakia in 1968? Chapuis makes not the slightest allusion! This kind of omission demonstrates the narrowness of the militant's vision, his factual ignorance, and the absence of reflection on the relationship between doctrine and politics in his book.

The second observation concerns the unbelievable naïveté of this man who never realizes for a moment that he reflects at every turn a sociological trend. In everything he says, he manifests his utter sociological conformity. This conformity also shows in his lack of knowledge and critical reflection (he criticizes only the hierarchy, on which he concentrates all his "lucidity"—since he obviously believes he is clairvoyant in this area). Chapuis is an excellent example of our earlier point concerning the obvious ideological primacy of socialism in our society. He never realizes that whereas he is justly critical of the model provided by Christendom (and here it is easy to be critical, since that Christendom is dead), he accepts utterly uncritically, and with good conscience, the exact equivalent of what Christendom was: we might call it "socialdom."

All Chapuis's choices are dictated by his milieu: the primacy of action, the scorn for theoretical discussion (he mistakes a few Marxist oversimplifications for theory), political commitment to the cause of the poor—as well as the identification of Christian faith with a new temporal order and the identification of revolution with the victory of the Left. In this astonishing conformity to the modern world, we observe the disappearance of the specificity of Christian consciousness. Chapuis's approach gives us a wonderful insight into the character that neo-Catholicism would have in France if it turned Communist.

Finally, we must consider certain aspects of Chapuis's doctrinal discussion. Right off the bat, he rejects, of course, the conflict between the Christian revelation of a Transcendent and Marxist materialism's obligation to exclude any Transcendent. In his rejection of the problem (without giving any explanation) he betrays still again his agreement with the prevailing trend.

I will mention only briefly Chapuis's series of factual historical errors: on pages 169-70, where he speaks of Church and Society in the Middle Ages and in modern times, the succession of errors bewilders: he makes ten factual errors (e.g., that Anglicanism comes out of the Reformed Church). In my opinion, his erudition is not at stake here. Chapuis's radically erroneous view of the character of the Church throughout history leads him to make false judgments and to stake out mistaken positions. Chapuis's unreliable history has a purpose, however: he gives us history just as it would be if Marxism were correct. Furthermore, he has a reason for beginning his historical section with a quotation from Gramsci that "clarifies" all these problems.

Besides these historical errors, Chapuis makes several remarkable mistakes concerning the present, such as: "By shattering the Marxist-socialist revolutionary movement, Hitler's or Mussolini's National Socialism left a wide-open field for the Church."[9] The reader thinks he is dreaming! The Church free under Hitler? Our author is oblivious to the most obvious facts (but they would do disservice to his argument).

We can also criticize Chapuis's generalization (p. 183) concerning "earlier" Christians' lack of political choice: "The very idea of a choice was refused them!" I find it unbelievable that he can be so ignorant of his Church's history! When he says that the nineteenth-century Catholic hierarchy imposed its point of view, we can agree. But when he generalizes, speaking of all eras, and identifies the Catholic hierarchy with "Christians," we are faced with enormous errors. Chapuis's labeling of Charles Péguy as a reactionary who harked back to the Middle Ages

---

9. Here we see that Chapuis does not bother with useless distinctions: National Socialism is the same as fascism, and Mussolini is a Nazi!

(p. 183) is also strange. He apparently fails to realize that Péguy was a socialist.

We must come to the central problem, however: in the descriptive section of his book, Chapuis speaks of the Church and Christians; then in the "doctrinal" section, suddenly he speaks of "faith." Faith in general, faith in itself; he does not explain the term. He omits Jesus Christ and the biblical revelation. We are left with just "faith." Faith that (by itself) moves mountains; what we have here is not the God of Jesus Christ who works a miracle promised when there is faith in this God of Jesus Christ! No—this is human faith, which can thus perfectly well be identified with the "courage and revolutionary will that makes tyrants fall" (p. 191). We have finally arrived, by eliminating any reference to the God of Jesus Christ: faith finally equals faith, and a Catholic can therefore be a Marxist with no problem. All content has been carefully eliminated: theology must give way to science. Chapuis gets rid of the problem through the death of God (p. 186).

He removes the content of faith by declaring it to be an ideology (p. 188). "Believing that Christ is God, that He became incarnate for the salvation of the human race" is an ideology—one that "we condemn today. . . . We have made our choice between the aristocratic sense of the saved person's superiority and the wretched action of the person trapped within history: between salvation and history, we choose history." And that's that: since Christianity no longer possesses any content, except for what can be assimilated to Marxist socialism, clearly the problem disappears.

Chapuis remains unperturbed by the fact that he thus strips away everything Scripture tells us about Jesus Christ. We can conclude with the following quotation, fit for an anthology:

> Am I or am I not a Christian at this point? Am I a Marxist or not? These are not my questions. Furthermore, if it were not for the needs of the political or civil religious state, such questions would hold little interest. To my way of thinking, the internal contradictions conveyed by the terms "Christian" and "Marxist" matter more than the relationships between them. This matter also fails to trouble me because I find myself confronted, as do other Christians and Marxists, by *much more important*

conflicts: between exploiters and those they exploit, between
modern means of domination and human efforts to achieve liberation from them.

Of course, the conflicts mentioned by Chapuis are very important; I have never minimized them.[10] Within this context, I
would criticize him for not recognizing the *genuine* conflicts of
our society, and for formulating them in terms of the nineteenth
century. But we must consider: what if this God, who is declared
dead, should be alive? What if He were the only Creator?[11] What
if Jesus were truly and fully God? What if He were really the
Savior of humanity and the Lord of history? What if God had
really revealed Himself? "That is no problem of mine," the
author replies smartly. No, unfortunately, your "problem" is
your chasing around like a nice little rabbit, down a wide-open
path you find well prepared and well lit—running around gives
the impression you are active. So you run faster and faster, with
all the other little rabbits. But at the end of the path, something
else is well prepared: the inevitable trap. And the rabbit realizes
his error too late; by then his long ears keep him from getting
out!

I would like to conclude simply with three observations.
(1) Christians have every reason for not being Communists.
They have almost no reason for being Communists. And yet we
observe the irresistible attraction Communism offers. We are

---

10. My severity in criticizing Chapuis should be considered in the context of the many points where I agree with him. In *The Presence of the Kingdom*, trans. Olive Wyon (Philadelphia: Westminster; London: SCM, 1951;
repr. New York: Seabury, 1967; French ed. 1948), I wrote of the "principle
of the laity" in almost the same terms Chapuis uses to formulate it. Also,
his "historical ethic" is similar to my position in *To Will and to Do: An Ethical Research for Christians*, trans. C. Edward Hopkin (Philadelphia: Pilgrim
Press, 1969). I also of course believe that worker management is a good
direction for struggle to take. But Chapuis formulates all these ideas in
such a way and with such commitment to Communist socialism that he actually abandons the content of revelation. He substitutes a socialist truth
for the truth of Jesus Christ and rationalizes his position as a Christian hos-
tage in the hands of the new ideological masters.

11. Another gem: "Only the people can be considered as creator; all
creation comes from the people!"

witnessing one of the most impressive of all sociological phenomena, extremely difficult to explain: how a sociopolitical
movement utterly opposed to a given social group manages to
acquire a power of attraction so strong that everyone joins up.
That includes those who should be the most hostile to the movement, who are condemned by it—but they are the first to get on
the bandwagon!

Christians in modern-day France offer an excellent example
of this sort of sociological obsession, amounting to a kind of
hypnosis or group psychology. No reasoning, argument, or experience can challenge such fascination. Moths are irresistibly
attracted by the light. I am reminded of B. Brecht's *The Resistible
Rise of Arturo Ui*. Naturally, seen from a distance and from the
outside, or in hindsight, we realize to what a degree this rise was
chancy and resistible! But in German society in 1932, it was irresistible; no reasoning or experience could stop it. And the
great majority of Christians were thoroughly in favor of it (the
"Confessing Church" amounted to a very small minority).

Presently we are seeing the same sort of joining up, which is
what makes the movement irresistible; it is not irresistible otherwise. I might add that the very fact that we see Christians fascinated in this way leads me to believe that the movement in question is implicitly totalitarian. And when it has won, it will show
itself explicitly to be totalitarian—even if there is no conscious
intention of this sort now.

My other two observations concern Christians, and consist
of an uncompromising reminder of two realities that have held
true throughout the history of Christianity. (2) Every time Christians have joined a political or social trend, prevailing or otherwise, we have always witnessed the deterioration of the faith
and Christian life. The result in every case has been adulteration
and corruption, even when it seemed at the outset that there was
a natural kind of affinity between the movement or doctrine involved and some aspect of revelation. The issue here is not
merely the (nonexistent!) "purity" of Christianity. We are dealing with the specific, irreplaceable vocation received by Christians from God. This vocation cannot be identified with anything else, and when Christians fail to live up to it, they are
utterly useless, and Christianity has no meaning.

(3) Any expression of revelation has a *radical critical role* with respect to all ideologies (especially prevailing ideologies!). There is no room for error regarding which ideology to criticize, or how to criticize it. For this we require a degree of lucidity which I find strangely lacking in those committed to this doubtful struggle!

Long ago I wrote an article trying to show the fundamental contradiction between Christianity and Communism. I received a long letter from a fine, devoted Protestant from southern France who believed I was utterly mistaken. He found an extraordinary harmony between the Communist and Christian ethic. The Communist ethic, including its tactics and strategy, expressed precisely what was being lived out in Christianity. What proof did he offer? He recommended I read the essential book by Liu Ch'ao-Chi, *How to Be a Good Communist*. Unfortunately, this devoted Protestant was writing early in 1966, a few months before the cultural revolution, in which Liu became public enemy number one, and his book was considered to be nothing but error!

Chapter III

Marginal Notes

1. Early Marxist-Christian Contact

A long time ago, around 1930, we wondered, along with A. Philipp, if it was possible to be both Christian and socialist (there was no question about being Christian and Marxist, and even less about combining Christianity and Communism!). We considered over and over conduct and ideas. We cared about God's justice, and therefore also about social justice. But what would best guarantee this social justice? And how could we take freedom for granted? Could socialism guarantee freedom? Certainly American freedom, seen at that time through the filter of assembly lines, mechanization at all levels, and unjust treatment of blacks, held no appeal for us.

Was it legitimate, however, to be so enthusiastic about political matters? In spite of G. Casalis's so-called discoveries (that Karl Barth had always been a socialist and that his theology had always been a political theology, poorly understood), Barth's followers were uninterested in the world's affairs. Some exceptions to this rule existed, especially D. de Rougemont, and a very few colorless followers. I was often lectured to back then so that I would see that everything is grace, that grace is sufficient, and that political matters are utterly without importance. The same people who lectured to me then have been proclaiming, since 1945, the primacy of politics, and often of Marx. Today they are still lecturing me—saying I am not sufficiently committed!

Those who strained to be both Christians and socialists in 1930 felt ill at ease and did not reconcile the differences easily. Then came the thunderbolt of 1938. Hitlerism moved even Christians with no political convictions toward socialism. Czechoslovakia led French Protestants to discover the extraor-

dinary importance of politics. Hitler's rise to power, the occupa-
tion of the Rhineland, rearmament, the persecutions of the
Jews—none of these things had previously upset our Protestant
intellectuals, and still less the theologians who speak importantly *today* of these questions!

Munich and Czechoslovakia, however, woke people up.
Protestants utterly ignorant of political matters declared themselves strongly anti-Munich—only five years too late. Great pan-
ics and crises occurred; the world was finally showing itself in
all its raw reality, and Christians tragically discovered they were
helpless. It seemed obvious to them, however, that politics was
a simple matter: that the ideas were clear and they could become
involved and make judgments that were as definitive as their refusal to make judgments had been a short while earlier. They had
no need to be acquainted with the questions raised by events.

Thus these Christians became enthusiastically involved in
the war against Hitler. A small problem was present, of course:
"love your enemies," and nonviolence, pacifism, and the like.
But we were given at last the explanation we needed: the whole
problem was reduced to the matter of love. That is, we had to
kill the Germans, but we must love them a great deal at the same
time. Make war but without hatred. That was the solution. I insist I am not exaggerating.

Today, again, we find exactly the same claim concerning
class struggle: it does not contradict love (on the contrary, as we
shall see). Naturally we must eliminate the vile proprietors, but
all the while loving them wholeheartedly. Apparently you could
even say it is for their own good that we strip them of their property, and even kill them, if necessary. The Church discovered
this formula long ago: heretics were burned for their own
good—for their salvation, that is. The current Christian
defenders of class struggle worthily carry on this tradition,
without realizing it, of course. In the same way, Christians in
World War II took their stand with a clear political conscience
and a more or less clear Christian conscience.

Beginning in 1941, with the Resistance, we witnessed the
great about-face. Our experience was two-edged: first, Hitlerism
was clearly evil; since the Soviet Union fought valiantly against
the Nazis, it represented the good. This basic judgment, a

simplistic position, was fundamental and determinative, in my view. Beginning at that time, Christian intellectuals and pastors declared that we must overcome our "narrow-minded" or "instinctive" anti-Communism. Even in 1950, these intellectuals and pastors failed to realize that they were the narrow-minded and instinctive ones, since they had scarcely any knowledge of Marx's thought, and none at all of Leninist-Stalinist tactics.

In the Resistance, then, we had the experience of comradeship and companionship with the Communists. Christians discovered that these Communists, whose name could be mentioned only uneasily just ten years earlier, were reliable companions: trustworthy, dedicated, scrupulous, human, and heroic. Prejudices evaporated! Communists were not intolerant or unfeeling. They were freedom fighters and victims. At this point our fine Christians discovered two things: whether one believed in God made little difference when it came to making correct political decisions, and that at last it was possible to do things (instead of being helpless).

It was not Christianity that rescued them from helplessness, however. It was their relationship with the Communists, who were experts in political action. Naturally, their relationship, once launched on the basis of mutual human understanding, moved onto the political level, where the Christians were open to being taught. But I insist that these were naïve Christians. They were sensitive to the Communists' human warmth and authenticity, their value statements, and at the same time they were utterly ignorant of the Party's structures, rigidity, and hidden dogmatism. They were utterly unprepared to criticize political ventures, and they were taken in by the heroism and effectiveness they witnessed. Clearly, in 1945, these Christians had no reason whatever to oppose Christianity and Communism. As for "Christianity and Marxism," it seemed a futile debate, without any real content, after the experience of the Resistance. The movement began based on this misunderstanding.

2. The "Death of God" and Marxism

We have already stated that it is too late to consider whether a materialist, anti-theistic philosophy can also be Christian. Until we have proof to the contrary, Christianity is not materialistic, and it affirms the existence of God. At least, it is too late to consider such a hybrid philosophy in the way it was considered a century ago, and as it is still considered by certain Catholic authorities.

Developments in this area, however, are significant: in the late 1950s, the Christians who would later become Marxists scoffed at this ridiculous issue, saying: "What? You are still looking for philosophical proofs? But look, that is no longer the issue! Considering Marxism to be opposed to Christianity is totally outdated. First, Marx's anti-theism is not an essential part of his doctrine; you have to look at the humanistic and economic sides of it. Second, materialism is a complicated issue. In the eighteenth or nineteenth century it made sense to struggle over the conflict between spiritualism and materialism. But surely you realize that back then they were attacking a simplistic view of Marx's materialism: a mechanistic view that gave physiological primacy to matter. But that is not what Marx says! This mechanistic view has nothing to do with his materialism, which is dialectical and social. Furthermore, you have to keep in mind that his materialism was directed against Hegelian idealism, and nothing else. So you can forget the whole outmoded debate over materialism. Joint effort to bring about justice and freedom is on a different level, and presupposes that reference to materialism or spiritualism is beside the point." This is how they spoke.

Things have changed since the late 1950s, however. First, we had the theologies of the death of God. Christians invented the idea. God is dead—utterly dead—we have nothing more to do with this "Father" who needs psychoanalyzing, this figurehead, this mythic personality, a ridiculous "Man Upstairs." Second, following the death of God, we had the discovery that everything is history. Of course. Everything depends on cultural factors, including expressions of faith, biblical texts, and the language of what was called revelation. But this discovery fitted in with the discovery that in the Old Testament we find an utterly materialistic concept of the person. Everything takes place on this earth: there is no afterlife. Death is final, and we are first and foremost a body. A "theology of the body" developed. The spirit (or conscience), of course, does not enter the picture until later, and it is connected to this body.

These two developments, the death of God and biblical materialism, took place quite independently of each other, but suddenly the light dawned, and the two were connected. Of course! If Christians are atheists, and matter is primary, then Marx was right! Christian truth requires an atheistic conclusion. Jesus came to teach us true atheism. Looking at it from another angle, one could ask, Who believes any longer that some ruling spirit could be the cause of matter? Hence, subscribing to Marx's philosophy no longer presented any problem. An amazing convergence took place.

Thus, in the first stage, when radical philosophical contradiction prevailed, we heard constantly that combining Marxism and Christianity poses no problem. At the second stage, once certain theological changes had taken place, a composite philosophy became possible. I believe these changes were made in good faith, with no Machiavellian intention of reaching an agreement with Marxism. But I also contend that they came about due to circumstances, and certainly not as a result of the Spirit's guidance! Once these theological conclusions are reached, suddenly the problem becomes very important, it takes the center of the stage, and we have everything to learn from Marx. We must learn our philosophy from him. Marxist atheism teams up perfectly with Christian atheism, and biblical materialism finds its perfect expression in Marx's materialism. This happy unity enables us to subscribe to both, since we have rediscovered, thanks to Marx, the authenticity of Christian revelation—after twenty centuries of obscurantist confusion! In other words, Marx's atheist, materialist positions became essential and central.

Later, however, we learned of many other such convergences: for example, that Christianity and Marxism are fundamentally related. P. Geoltrain (in *Réforme*, April 1978) reminds us that E. Käsemann points out "a profound affinity between Marxism and Christianity, owing to certain fundamental biblical insights." Seeing Marxism as a kind of secularized Christianity is hardly new—the idea dates from the beginning of the twentieth century.

No doubt Marx adopts (unconsciously!) the whole outline: Eden, the Fall, sin, the Redeemer, redemption, the Parousia, etc. He calls these "the primitive society, commodity and false consciousness, alienation, the proletariat, the proletarian revolution, and Communist society." None of this has anything whatever to do, however, with explaining the fundamental *religious* nature of Marxism. The central issue is unrelated to this "biblical" outline; it hinges on Marx's personal contribution. In particular, we must note that in Marx redemption is not accomplished by assuming the greatest possible weakness and through willing sacrifice, undertaken as God's will. Rather, redemption in Marx comes through the conquest of power, violent action, uniting forces, and physical triumph over the enemy. This enemy is by no means surrounded with love; he is loathed and killed.

We must not paper over these differences by speaking only of solidarity with the poor! In Marxist dialectic, the oppressed must become oppressors. So we cannot limit ourselves to doing what Christians have always done in their political involvements: submit to the present circumstances and resolutely close our eyes to the outcome and future consequences. We are invited to take just such a blind leap when urged to subscribe here and now to the struggle on behalf of the poor, understood in terms of world Communism!

3. Theology of Service, Theology of the Poor, Horizontal Theology

The theological process that led to Marxist Christianity is complex. The theology of the death of God, mentioned above, which played a philosophical role, is an exception. We can simply note that this theology is no longer taken seriously today. It is usually considered outmoded, having run its course. We need to realize that this theology was eliminated *after* it had its sociological effect. It was presented at first as a new understanding of revelation—a fundamental theological discovery, a renewal of all theology. But it was just a lubricant so that Marx's atheism could slide in—then this theology went up in smoke.

In place of the theology of the death of God, other doors

opened: the theology of service, for instance. This theology insisted that Christianity in its entirety was limited to, summed up in, service. We had done too much talking; it was time to act. We had to leave verbal love behind and move on to actions: "Not every one who *says* to me, 'Lord, Lord'" (Matt. 7:21). We needed to remember that everything comes down to service (and both Greek *leitourgia* and *diakonia* mean "service"). When you have served your neighbor, you have served God. Anyone who does not love his brother does not love God. In this way, the theology of service started from the clear, basic principle we must call to mind with radical insistence, that good works are the fruit of faith, and that no one can claim to confess and love Jesus Christ unless he expresses his faith in his life.

However, the theology of service was not the same as this important principle, which was just one part of an overall theology. As always, deviation occurred; the principle got off the track: service was taken to be sufficient in itself. It became everything. Love is testified to adequately in the service you render. Speech is vain and superfluous. Speech is subject to all sorts of misunderstandings and confusion; *speaking* about Jesus Christ means nothing. Pronouncing His name amounts to magic. Even worse: if you state that you serve in the name of Jesus Christ, this means you have the dreadful intention of converting another person.

You must render a pure, selfless service, and if you have conversion in mind, you are guilty of proselytizing (like the nuns did for so long, taking advantage of people's illness, etc.). You do not truly love your neighbor, you merely want to add his scalp to your collection. In this light, it would be better to avoid any possible confusion and not say anything at all about Jesus Christ. You must accept your neighbor just as he is, without influencing him. So what if he fails to become a "Christian"? On the contrary, you must see things from his perspective, put yourself in his shoes, instead of trying to attract him to your position. You must follow the person in need of service everywhere—no matter where he goes. You must not consider your own welfare; you must love him enough to risk losing yourself. Service must be all-out, and it is enough in itself—service theology went to this extreme.

The theology of service joined forces with the theology of the poor and gave it added strength. We need not review the point of departure for the theology of the poor: the admirable and essentially correct rediscovery that Jesus came in poverty, lived with and for the poor, and that the God of Jesus is not a Jupiter who thunders but the humble God who became human and a servant. These rediscoveries led to another: "the eminent dignity of the poor."

Again, in this case, however, a deviation occurred very quickly: the principle got off the track, as always happens. Theologians moved from the above essential truth to poisonous language. Concretely, they overemphasized the famous warning in the parable of the sheep and the goats (Matt. 25:31ff.), which became, between 1960 and 1970, the central text for all of theology. This text summed up the entire gospel: serving the poor as their poverty demands (without witnessing to Jesus Christ) constitutes our entire service to God.

Thus the poor person is identified with Jesus Himself, beginning with the parable of Matthew 25. Soon the deviation takes a more serious turn. In an amazing fashion, the poor person becomes the absolute, a kind of priest: he is the intermediary, the mediator. Only through him can we meet Jesus and God; through serving him we are sanctified. The poor person is a veritable sacrificial victim. Furthermore, in his action as a poor individual he accomplishes here and now the will of God in history. This is precisely the role of the priest, in whom eternity and time are joined together. Francis of Assisi's statement about priests is applied almost word for word to the poor: "I pay no heed to their sins, because I see the very Son of God in them, and they are my teachers." Today's theology of the poor is a theology of a new priesthood.

In the next step, the convergence of the theology of the death of God, the theology of service, and the theology of the poor (in all their distortions and excesses) produces what is called "horizontal theology." No point in looking for someone to answer us from heaven: everything takes place on earth. No point in lifting our eyes to heaven, as the angels point out (Acts 1:11). No point in believing in unusual powers: "They glorified God, who had given such authority to *men*" (Matt. 9:8). The human dimension is the only one. Faith is faith in humanity. The only knowledge of God is knowledge of people, just as the only service of God is service to people. The resurrection is the continuation of Jesus' message by means of insurrection. No point in considering transcendence; and, of course, we no longer use the symbolism of the cross with its vertical and horizontal axes. We can skip lightly over the matter of the two greatest commandments: the second one suffices.

Such ideas eerily recall Feuerbach's philosophy. Even more strangely, the inventors of this horizontal theology seem never to have suspected that they merely repeated what Feuerbach had said one hundred fifty years earlier. Or that, like him, they were trying to save Christianity by freeing it from faith in Christ and the Father, by putting humanity in God's place (this was Marx's criticism of Feuerbach).

We have seen how each of these three theologies (of the death of God, of service, and of the poor) began by discovering a truth, only to fall victim to a deviation. In the case of horizontal theology, we need not try to pinpoint the deviation, since we are clearly dealing with a theology without foundation, from its very start. Rather, its only foundation is sentimentalism or a strictly human ideology.

We can make a significant observation, however: the three errors on which horizontal theology is based come down to the same, undeclared principle: "This" is sufficient in itself. Service suffices by itself (it need not *receive* its dignity or value from Jesus). The historical Jesus is sufficient by Himself (He need not receive His truth from a Father or from God). "Sufficient unto itself!" Here we have the essence of heresy: for the proclamation that the self (even of the poor person) is sufficient contradicts love. Such sufficiency amounts to the negation of Jesus—even if one is speaking about the poor! We must remember that the poor person fulfills his true mission only by the love of God, never by himself.

Horizontal theology, a result of the three others, completes the circle, so that a person is enclosed within a system that has no exit. He sees nothing opposite him except himself. He is absolutely alone on earth. Divinity is within him, it is himself. No help will come to him from beyond the hills, for he has closed the gate of the gods. He has enclosed himself theologically within Babel (strangely enough, moreover, one of the champions of horizontal theology tries to rehabilitate Babel). In other words, horizontal theology returns quite simply to the project of excluding God, just as the Bible carefully describes it, using the leitmotif of the city.[1]

Since the little fellow can now protest loudly (theologically) that he is sufficient unto himself, he must find a new hope (in humanity), and an end (for history). Thus horizontal theologians delightedly seized not at all the biblical hope (since they wanted nothing to do with an afterlife), but an earthly, historical philosophy of hope. They refused to hear the Word of God, but listened with pleasure to E. Bloch and his promises. Since no eschatological hope of resurrection exists, and humanity must do everything by itself, an end and meaning must be found for this history within history. Revolution and humanity's self-liberation will inevitably provide such significance. For this purpose we replace spiritual reflection with plays on words, so that resurrection becomes insurrection; then etymological insurrection becomes historical insurrection—in other words, revolution.

Thus the first step is taken through the gate of revolution, which forms the premise of liberation. Liberation theologies form the next step, based, of course, on a theological argument: if God is the Liberator, the gospel is a gospel of liberation. But God intervenes in history only through human hands. Thus humankind must liberate itself. At this point, no need bothering with anything further: we can safely sail on the high sea of human political actions. Liberation is a human affair. That is, it has to do with all oppressed people, believers or unbelievers. If they are oppressed, that suffices. Politics is the means of liberation. We abandoned nonpolitical slavery along the way. This is a strange development, yet fundamentally understandable: humanity is alone on the earth, so that its future depends on its own efforts. What if, by some chance, tragically, people were evil, weak, and corrupted? What if, by some terrible chance,

---

1. On this theme, I refer the reader to my work on the theology of the city: *The Meaning of the City*, trans. Dennis Pardee (Grand Rapids: Eerdmans, 1970).

they were basically sinners, as the Bible says? Such a thing is inconceivable! It would mean instant suicide. At this point, without remorse (psychoanalysis helps us here), we explain the purely illusory and mythological origin of this "notion" of sin. No, people are neither corrupted nor sinners. They are basically good. Only an erroneous understanding of the biblical text could make us believe otherwise. Humanity is merely alienated, stripped of its essential being by economic and political structures. Simply by eliminating this alienation, humanity will return to its essential nature (we gloss carefully over the fact that such alienation must have its source in other people, who must not be as good as all that; but we must quickly forget this).

Liberation is thus simply a political matter, on humanity's level. After all, we are beginning to understand that psychological abnormalities result either from the trauma of a vitiated education or from subhuman living conditions. Give a person his political freedom, and he will be good. The trick, then, is to express through political liberation the liberation symbolically attributed to God. But in any case, liberation has only a political dimension. Conversely, no liberation can take place without political liberation. Faith, hope, God's Kingdom, prayer—all are abominable evasions that have only enabled the ruling class to demand obedience and to keep the oppressed from revolting.

The only reality that counts is this *earthly, political, here-and-now* liberation. Everything else is rubbish. We are people who think clearly; we have our feet on the ground (we used to add, "and our head in heaven"; unfortunately, our head is also now on ground level). We are not taken in by fairy tales; in any case, with the advent of structuralist and psychoanalytical interpretations, fairy tales have also served to expose the horror of the ruling class's exploitation. Starting from this theology of liberation, we move on, without flinching, of course, to Marxist Christianity. The two are clearly identical: only Marxists work for human liberation, so we must work with them to carry out the promise of the gospel. We must work with the Marxists, digest their thinking, and identify ourselves with their action and interests—and with no one else's.

I am left speechless by the fact that after such thinking people still feel the need to do theology and to use Jesus as a reference point. I cannot understand why such a cumbersome presence seems useful. Since revolution is the essential matter, get on with it, instead of encumbering yourselves with such roundabout oratory and rationalization. Since politics is the essential matter, get on with it, instead of obstinately sticking with theology.

What does "theology" mean, anyway? Why "theo" at all, since you talk of nothing but politics and human beings? All you believe in is a sort of god brought down to earth, in humankind and within history. What is the point of struggling to probe this pseudo-word of a pseudo-god? Why use Jesus at all? Any hero of a popular liberation would do just as well. Why use this old document for reference, when Marx stands on his own so well? Since you insist Christian faith offers nothing specific, why do you want to hang onto these old rags at all costs?

Are you trying to change Jesus into one of those nineteenth-century-style "models"? But back then, Jesus was a *moral* model, whereas now you would make Him a political one. "His political practice is exemplary," you say. Let's try to understand each other. Two options exist: on the one hand, if Jesus really took His place in opposition to the powers, in such a way that His action cannot be identified with *any* other, present-day action, then the Christian has a specific action to carry out. He says what no one else can say, and acts like no one else. On the other hand, a Christian can adopt the vocabulary, analyses, explanations, and commitments of Marxism; in this case he identifies himself with the oppressed *as Marxism designates and defines them.* He takes part in the action proposed by the Marxists, disavowing any Christian specificity. In this case, why hang onto the cumbersome "model"?

Jesus clearly gets in the way, judging from the terribly labored exegetical and theological contortions these philosophers of liberation and revolutionary praxis go through. To prove that class struggle existed in Jesus' time, that He was the political chief of the exploited masses, etc., they have to twist the texts unbelievably. They must resort to dizzying intellectual acrobatics, usually resting their case on mere word variants. It is another case of torturing Jesus to make Him fit our confining categories.

How much simpler it would be not to deal with all this! But our Marxist Christians would not dream of abandoning their faith; they feel a sentimental attachment to God's revelation, and would suffer traumatically if they eliminated the label from their lives. They prefer to reconcile and rationalize. Falling prey to a process repeated throughout history, they claim to safeguard Christianity's authenticity by selecting from it those elements that can be made to coincide with the prevailing ideological movement of the day: in this case, Marxism. Ignorant of history, they fail to realize that this process has been tried a thousand times, for the purpose of restoring Christianity's authenticity. Always it has appeared extremely helpful, but without fail it has produced catastrophe for faith and the revelation. How much better it would be to blot out the Bible and Christ, abandon them once and for all, and thus be able to limit one's efforts to "serious matters": politics, the economy, revolution, the Third World, and the oppressed classes.

Nothing very new or startling is involved in proclaiming the Christian call as revolutionary in all areas. One can declare the gospel to be a revolutionary message, but the Old Testament's message is just as revolutionary. Obviously this revolution involves all levels: political, economic, cultural, spiritual, moral, and intellectual: "Do not be conformed to this world" (Rom. 12:2). But we must refuse to conform to the world in its totality. We cannot say "within this world there are positive aspects we will preserve." In other words, the revelation requires us to recast everything in terms other than those used by *all* the trends in society.

Christians have continually rediscovered and reaffirmed this truth, in the midst of a thousand contradictions, as we all know. Christians became unrepentant revolutionaries in the second, fourth, eighth, and twelfth centuries, as well as at other times. Arrogant and impudent accusations that the Church has always sided with the powerful and supported the state and the ruling classes amount to abominable historical lies. Accepting the Marxist lie about the Church in this fashion implies that the Church has always been a perfectly unified whole, exercising a single function with just one doctrine!

In *The Presence of the Kingdom*, published about twenty years before the birth of the theologies of revolution and liberation,[2] I showed that revolutionary Christianity has been recast in our time. In it I formulated the radical call to revolutionary Christianity. True, my emphasis differed from current efforts: in *The Presence of the Kingdom* I showed that Christian revelation leads to a new understanding of revolution. We must be revolutionary *because* we are Christians. Now, with Christianity absorbed by Marxism, the emphasis is rather on being revolutionary while remaining Christian (in spite of everything, as an exceptional case, covered with all sorts of apologies).

At this point we return to my previous argument: revolutionary Christianity, the Christian option of revolution, acted out its historical role each time and failed in the end. It failed exactly as every revolution has failed since history began (but *after* playing its role). It failed, furthermore, as a Christian revolutionary option. Each specific failure stemmed not from some horrible repression exercised by the ecclesiastical institution, but from the impossibility of making history bring about the Kingdom of God. We must be content with living out, here and now, within the world's reality, the revolution of the Kingdom of Heaven. It never attains a "Christian" society nor an order of things after God's own heart.

As specifically revolutionary and because of revelation, Christians *also* necessarily adopt the revolutionary tendencies of their time. Christian socialists? Why not, provided they understand that socialism is far from revolutionary, that it tends to solve social problems dating from a century ago (a very necessary task, to be sure!). They must recognize that socialism fails to discern, and in any case could not solve, our new challenges and alienations. Christians must be able to discern these new situations; as I have often written, such discernment constitutes the specifically revolutionary task of Christians. "Brothers, we must rise to strike out on paths no one has ever before mapped out or even recognized."

---

2. Originally published as *Présence au monde moderne* (Geneva: Roulet, 1948); Eng. trans. by Olive Wyon: *The Presence of the Kingdom* (Philadelphia: Westminster, 1951; repr. New York: Seabury, 1967).—TRANS.

For Christians to be socialists, then, poses no obstacle, so long as they realize there is nothing revolutionary in such a stance. But Marxist Christians are another matter—they amaze and baffle me! Not simply because Marxism also deals with outdated social and economic situations (as socialism does), but primarily because Marxism offers, whether we like it or not, an overall philosophy: an explanation of the world, humanity, history, etc. Apparently our repeated historical experience as Christians has taught us nothing.

Christians are continually tempted by syncretism, which each historical period revives. Sometimes a philosophy emerges to attract society's great minds. At other times a new politics surfaces, mustering the forces of a people. At other periods a new concept develops that finally offers an explanation for humanity's condition and problems. Or a force will appear that belongs clearly to the future, and may engulf everything in its path. The Christians on the scene are a poor little Church, which is extremely fragile and marginal, because of its authenticity. They possess no effective means of changing society, no overall system of thought; they are always defenseless, dependent on grace, which might, after all, let them down, they think. They are grounded in the Word, but it could, after all, fall silent, they reason. They must proclaim this Word to every creature, and all peoples will recognize the Lord as the only God. Thus the temptation comes along to unite with this rising force that is so very human, containing within itself all humanity's wisdom, intelligence, greatness, and future.

Plato attracts us. We must manage a synthesis, and the prevailing gnosticisms seem so close to what we believe that they make off in their wake with hundreds of thousands of believers at a time. Why not join their orbit? The emperor experiences a genuine Christian conversion; why not align ourselves with this earthly justice, this true search for power that bows down before the true God? Aristotle appears with all the knowledge that assembled human intelligence has managed to gather; how can Christianity remain aloof from such a magnificent human development? Here comes the bourgeoisie, apparently so concerned with strict morality, with truth that goes beyond ritual and superstitions, beyond the suspicious ambiguities of faith and piety so corrupted by demonism. The bourgeoisie searches for clarity and reasonableness. How could Christianity fail to go along with this demand?

Each time Christians followed these paths they adulterated their faith and the revelation. They either twisted Scripture or forgot it, in order to subscribe to the wise discoveries and profit from the great possibilities confronting them. Naturally, a century or two later, the enormity of their error became obvious. And it was so easy to condemn one's dead ancestors, who could not defend themselves.

Each time the process has been exactly the same: Christians were attracted by what seemed obvious in a movement of their time. At first they would approach with caution; then they would struggle passionately to bring revelation into line with the current taste, and finally they would bring to it the foundation, means, strengths, and certitudes it so obviously lacked.

Presently Marxist Christians reveal that they are going through an identical process. Marx takes the place of Plato or Aristotle, the proletarian masses substitute for the emperor or the bourgeoisie, but the operation is strictly identical. Each time Christians believe that they have at last found a blinding light that enables them to understand the essence of their message (they always look for the light on the outside!). Like Marx today, Plato or Aristotle clarified at last what God had said.

How enlightening, for example, to understand now, thanks to Althusser, that the dogma of the Trinity is a clear reflection of bourgeois ideology.[3] At last we can enter, trembling, the mysteries of knowledge, by demythologizing it. But we can also see where all this leads, unfortunately. We are not seeing the liberation of humanity, the greatest truth of the gospel, nor the explanation of history. Instead, the end result will be another instance of the radical betrayal of the Unique One and His Word, culminating in a clouding of it, and the fusion of Christians with a large movement that will shortly expel them.

---

3. This kind of pernicious analysis ends up defeating itself. I could easily demonstrate that Althusser's thought boils down to a mere reflection of the Technological System, utterly without originality.

4. Liberation Theologies and Marxist Christians

Can Christians be in favor of socialism? Of course! But the question "Which socialism?" arises immediately. Are you for F. Fourrier, P. Proudhon, or K. Marx? For libertarian socialism, utopian socialism, or scientific socialism? More to the point, do you mean social democracy, Swedish socialism, Egyptian socialism, or Indonesian socialism? Such awkward details never enter the endless waves of Christian discourse on socialism, in which socialism is recognized as having indisputable value, since it is the manifestation of Christian incarnation.

Those who clearly opt for Marxism immediately take refuge in a nebulous socialism. Some speak as if socialism were automatically identical with Marxism; they view Marxism as the only conceivable representative of socialism. Others start out talking about Marxism and Marxist Communism, but then prefer to beat a retreat to socialism, since it scares fewer people off and helps the pill go down easier. These, too, fail to give details, they hesitate, they touch on the subject ever so lightly, so that we can never know what such experts mean when they say "socialism."

For many, being "socialist" is part of their being, a form of reaction. Pick up a publication such as *Réforme* (a French Protestant weekly), for instance; nearly everything in it suggests socialism, without ever saying anything about it explicitly. Being socialist means denouncing apartheid, colonialism, and imperialism; siding with oppressed people, feminists, homosexuals, and the young against the old (all the while expressing teary-eyed concern for the elderly); pleading the cause of immigrant workers; struggling against requiring too fast a pace of industrial employees, and struggling for raising the minimum wage; attacking Israel's imperialism, etc. Socialism boils down to these matters, more or less. But we are not given any serious reflection. We can never know the basis of a given stance, or what direction it wants to take us. All we have are rather vague principles: siding with the oppressed and fighting for justice.

As we have noted, however, some make an apparently clearer choice: socialism as the equivalent of Marxism. But in reality, their stance also remains fuzzy. I need not repeat here what I alluded to in the preceding chapter concerning the rainbow of

Marxist doctrinal options. It is as extensive as the socialist range. But what does it mean then to call oneself a Marxist? Subscribing to the thought of Marx himself? But which thought? Marx before or after his well-known "epistemological shift"?

Furthermore, you are considered pedantic if you refer in such detail to Marx's thought. Such examination is all right for specialists, but not for militants. As a very committed Communist student said to me one day as he was leaving one of my classes on Marx, "After all, I really don't see why we should study Marx's thought. A lot I care about Marx! You don't need that to be a Communist." His chin stiffened to underscore his feelings. I get the impression that many Marxist Christians would say the same thing. Some of them cling to a rough idea of Marx drawn from the philosophical approach to history; others reject that philosophy but hold to the historical analysis of economic evolution and its consequences in socialist society. For many others, Marxism is "science." But at this point we have lost touch with our starting point: we are dealing with Marxism rather than Marx.

In this light, we had best delve no further into the countless ramifications of all the contradictory Marxisms. Some Marxist Christians, however, scorn all these doctrines and discussions fit for intellectuals: the important thing is to be committed. Being a Marxist means joining the Communist Party (but why the Communist Party rather than the Trotskyite League or the Maoist movements?). It involves first and foremost working together. Being a Marxist means standing shoulder to shoulder in demonstrations, petitions, etc. All Marxists, however, hold to class struggle as part of their platform. (We will return to this principle.) Many also hold to materialism. But this brings us back to where we started, to uncertain ground.

I have no intention of raising trick questions, or of entering the philosophical debate we have seen to be outmoded. Rather, I want to consider the great diversity of expressions concerning this materialism. For some, their understanding has to do with Marxism as science. They apply this materialism with strictness, then; we will study several examples of this application, but I cannot see the difference between this sort of materialism and the simple application of the classical historical method. This goes for exegesis (historical-critical) as well as for interpretation. You can read these texts, trying to imagine what H. Taine or M. Weber or even A. de Tocqueville would have said differently, on the same issue. On this score, no one is a more thoroughgoing Marxist than P. Chaunu! In this case, where Marxism is understood as science, "materialism" simply means "careful work."

For others, materialism means primarily the rehabilitation of the body, which, they believe, Christianity despised, repressed, and banished. They identify all of Christianity with Molière's Tartuffe, the hypocrite. Apart from the error involved in this accusation, we must remember that Marx was utterly hostile to this sort of materialism, which is the materialism of the eighteenth century, of the Baron d'Holbach and J. de La Mettrie. Marx insisted on breaking with these tendencies, so that being Marxist has nothing to do with pleading the cause of the body, the primacy of the corporeal, the body's needs and requirements, as opposed to the spirit.

If by materialism one means challenging the idealist evasion, then no problem exists: no Christian will take issue with that sort of materialism. Scripture teaches the unity of the person. But most of the time, materialism amounts to affirming the primacy of "matter," so that the body precedes and determines the "spirit" (Marx used the term "consciousness"). Economic activity determines class relationships, and they determine everything else.

This primacy of matter would obscure the possibility of a creation by a transcendent God who "precedes" matter. The materialist would prefer to gloss over this problem. But there is an additional difficulty: the Spirit's action could not be produced by class struggle. Materialism would reject that the spirit can be a determinative force, that the Holy Spirit's action is expressed in the biblical text, that spiritual inspiration precedes commitment in concrete social situations, that the spiritual life can also be full and authentic in a monastery of prayer where no social intervention takes place, that truth resides in the person of Jesus, not because He participates in the class struggle, but because He is the Son of the Eternal God, and is Himself God and precedes the creation. The Kingdom comes by the miracle of the Spirit rather than through economic history. Materialism rejects these and many other Christian affirmations. Although not always stated explicitly, these contradictions are clear for certain Marxist Christians. But their discretion is such that we have difficulty understanding their reinterpretation of biblical teaching.

For the majority, however, "materialism" is not so strict; it amounts to a mere protest intended to make Christians take socioeconomic and political activity seriously. In this case I have no difficulty agreeing with them; I would even accept applying a Marxist analysis to *these* areas. I have been pleading this cause for forty years, but it has nothing to do with materialism.

For most Marxist Christians, the main issue is limited to class struggle. This is their litany:

Litany

Human life on earth is what matters.
Anything else constitutes a refusal to see reality.
Reality is identical with truth.
Human reality in our world and time is alienation.
Human alienation is the fault of bourgeois imperialist
    capitalism.
People's poverty stems from their alienation.
Jesus became poor. He reveals Himself only in His poor, earthly
    condition.
We know nothing of Him except for the recollection of that
    poverty.
Jesus identified Himself with the poor.
Every poor person is Jesus Himself.
Every poor person must be defended.
    If we fail to defend him, we attack him.
Failing to struggle on behalf of the poor
    means we reject Jesus.
Hypocrisy avoids this struggle by looking to the Beyond.
    To Heaven.
Any sort of vertical relationship with God is hypocrisy,
    and scorns Jesus.
Jesus never referred to a transcendent God.
The powerful and the exploiters created a transcendent God
    in their image.
God is not transcendent, not eternal, not all-powerful, not Lord,
    not the Father.
This God is dead, since all of God is revealed in Jesus
    as a poor person.

If God is dead, then what matters is human life on earth.
The death of God is the liberation of humanity.
This struggle for liberation is the only spiritual reality.
The ruling class prevents people from being liberated.
Jesus participated in class struggle, since He assumed the entire
    human condition.
Only those who participate in this struggle are true to Jesus.
All those who work for human liberation are true to Jesus,
    whatever their methods.
The Communist Party dedicates itself to class struggle.
Jesus' faithful followers should therefore participate
    in the Party's struggle.
By participating in class struggle, we truly meet Jesus.
Through this class struggle, Jesus confirms that human life
    on earth is what matters.

That settles everything. Each sentence fits in perfectly with the preceding one. Furthermore, you can begin this litany at any point, and its meaning remains intact. It is the same old story over and over again.

Marxist Christians like to talk about liberation. So do I. But we do not say exactly the same thing. Fine theologies of liberation have been constructed, but I prefer to speak of an ethic of freedom. The only person to give our modern age a complete understanding of freedom is Bernard Charbonneau, who is utterly unknown. This fact shows clearly that freedom does not interest anyone, contrary to politicians' and intellectuals' contentions.

Freedom has at long last been formally readopted as one of the Left's values. As I continually remind people, in 1945 and even in 1950, those who mentioned the word "freedom" were automatically labeled Rightists—and fascists at that. Back then, our friends the Marxists were all Stalinists; and our present Marxist Christians were addicted to the personality cult. They were touchier than anyone concerning the authenticity of Communism in the Soviet Union. We need not press this issue.

Today, then, the grand theme of freedom has been retrieved. We must free the proletariat, the poor, the exploited. Examples: the intensity of the struggle in favor of the Vietcong against the colonialists, and then the Vietnamese struggle against the rotten imperialist regime of Saigon, and finally the Khmer Rouge struggle against the rotten imperialist regime of Phnom Penh. I can still remember the lovely graffiti on all French campuses: "The Indochinese people will be victorious. Freedom for the people of Indochina."

Today the imperialists and their capitalism have left, but the slavery of all these peoples is a thousand times more agonizing and inhuman than the worst colonialism ever was. But no one is interested in them anymore. Our Marxist Christians turn out as soon as they hear of any police action in Soweto or any hypothetical or possible torture in Israel, but the execution of a million people in Cambodia leaves them cold. The enslavement of 90% of South Vietnam's population by the Tonkinese no longer interests them. Once the Western white capitalist colonialist imperialists have been driven out, all is well.

As soon as we hear someone mention the word "liberation" today, we must listen carefully and ask at least one pointed question. Not the traditional question, "liberation from what—what force, oppression, or slavery?" The problem no longer lies there. Rather, we must ask "liberate . . . *for whose benefit?*" Who will be the new oppressor, the new master?

We must systematically destroy the childish ideology that follows this pattern: "Where you have a dictator and an oppressed people, kill the dictator to liberate the people. They will organize themselves and become their own masters. They will come of age and enter into their freedom" (at this point, since the unexamined goal has been attained, no reason remains for trying to ascertain what really happened).

Facts show that no people in the world ever found freedom after going through its "war of liberation" (from capitalism and imperialism). No Arab, African, or Asiatic people has come to the faintest glimmer of freedom in this manner. On the contrary, they all lost whatever remained of their freedom before their "liberation." We can say, without any fear of proof to the contrary, that these peoples are *all* presently less free and less happy than they were under colonial domination. Never did they have so many police, prisons, and political executions. Their only bitter satisfaction is that now at least the dictatorship oppressing them is homegrown. At least those putting them in prison and assassinating them are their own compatriots.

"For whose benefit, this liberation?" If we fail to ask this question, we are either hypocritical or naïve. But this is precisely the question that never comes up in our brilliant theologies of liberation or revolution. Things are always wonderfully clear: on the one hand you have the poor, the oppressed, the exploited, and on the other hand the capitalist imperialists. Do away with the latter, side with the former (a Christian's duty), and, miraculously, liberation takes place. But this miracle is the result of the historical revolutionary action of the people themselves—a genuine resurrection of the people. We can end the matter here.

Liberation theologies unfortunately perpetuate the characteristics of the most despicable traditional theologies! For one thing, they remain amazingly abstract, in spite of their concrete appearance. Their abstraction consists of not asking the decisive concrete question ("liberation for whose benefit?"). In the same way the bourgeois theologies of the seventeenth to nineteenth centuries were abstract. Yet they appeared concrete, since they all led to such a practical moral code! In exactly the same way our liberation theologies lead to political strategies and tactics for liberation! Bourgeois theologians carefully avoided asking the question, "For whose benefit do we prescribe these individual virtues, sacrifices, and proper conduct?" Theirs was an abstract theology, since it failed to question bourgeois capitalism concretely. Today liberation theologies are abstract in that they fail to question socialist or Communist dictatorships where a tiny minority exercises power over a people more enslaved than ever.

Liberation theologies also perpetuate traditional theologies in a second way: they rationalize, just like the theologies of the seventeenth to nineteenth centuries. Back then, theology served to justify the building of the capitalist system; today it justifies "revolutionary" and socialist undertakings. Thus liberation theologies have not changed theology's role: their changed content stems only from a changed political and economic situation, and from the Church's different place within that evolution.

We must understand each other, however. I do not suggest for a moment that these movements are unnecessary or avoidable. I am well acquainted with the wretched condition of

Latin America's peasant populations, the insane exploitation of its workers, and the excesses of all political systems in all countries: torture, police, etc. I know as much as the next person about the United States' intervention, the huge fruit and mining companies. Consequently the will to fight these oppressions is perfectly normal, and its aspiration is just.

Surely no one could side with what is taking place in Latin America or condemn its revolutionary movements? We must harbor no illusions, however. Once victorious, the revolution will not remain in the hands of a liberated people. Instead, it will fall into those of a dictator or a fierce party, just as oppressive as the previous torturer (for we must not romanticize Cuba and good old Castro, the hail-fellow-well-met!). In this combat, the so-called liberation theologies are political theologies partial to one side (the poor!), so that in the last analysis they end up justifying the future dictatorship. We know in advance that once the Left has won, no matter what its actions, the theologies of liberation will paper over the coming slavery without batting an eye.

In other words, as a tool of propaganda here and now, in *this* particular revolutionary conflict, at *this* stage, these theologies have a certain value, even a legitimacy. But they amount to nothing more than propaganda. They in no way contribute to the advance of theology, faith, or worship. And since they are merely the expression of a particular historical situation, that of today's Amerindian world, they cannot spread elsewhere and serve as a model or inspiration for African or Western theologies.

Although many follow the road from Jesus to Marx these days, some follow the road from Marx to Jesus. Take the example of Roger Garaudy. He has taken such a long route that I am not sure whether we can still call him a Marxist. In any case, he does not belong to the Christian-Marxist element. Garaudy knows Marx's thought too well to attempt to reinterpret Christianity in terms of Marx.

We should make at least one remark concerning Garaudy: not concerning his books, but based on his short "Confession of Faith" (*Le Monde*, June 1978), a very significant article, since it deals with the debate over "faith." The author establishes several postulates that are logically acceptable (each person is responsible for his life, has an open future, must empty himself, since the negative approach is essential, etc.). We could call these postulates *of faith*, the postulates of all revolutionary action—faith as the experience of origins.

In all of this Garaudy means to legitimize faith as a human psychological, intellectual, existential attitude. "Faith" has value in itself and gives meaning. But here we are at the level of the human, of psycho-spiritual experience. The amazing thing about this attitude (the utterly common attitude of the nineteenth century and the beginning of the twentieth) is its ability to separate faith from its object. Faith, after all, necessarily involves a relationship: without a second term (what one believes in, the subject or object of faith, what one's confidence or faithfulness applies to, etc.), faith is not present.

Garaudy's interest, however, is precisely the possibility and validity of faith *in itself*. But we have no trouble understanding that faith has reality only in terms of what characterizes it: the attitude is the same, but everything changes, depending on what one has faith in. As far as the faith is concerned, faith in Hitler is the same as faith in Jesus Christ; yet the life springing from it is utterly different. Legitimizing the attitude of faith, as Garaudy attempts it, is not essential; rather, we must know the reference of this faith. Saying just "faith" amounts to saying nothing.

When Garaudy speaks of God, he says, somewhat flippantly, "I use the word 'God' because others have used it, but I do not need it to express my faith. All I know of God is the action of those who bear witness to him." Thus we have "the immense faith of the world," and then an individual case, Jesus, who showed how one can live a human life divinely. So we have faith, and then a special witness to faith.

Garaudy neglects, however, the whole matter of faith in this Jesus Christ, as something unique and qualitatively different from all other faith. The New Testament emphasizes not faith, but Jesus Christ, in whom we should place all our confidence and certainty, by whom we receive, through the intermediary of faith, forgiveness and salvation. Jesus Christ matters, not faith. He determines faith, not vice versa. He makes us Christians, not the existence of our faith! Otherwise, the whole soteriological dimension of Jesus' death disappears, along with its messianic dimension and the unfolding of the Kingdom. It is not a human kingdom, not based on faith in humanity, and not the realization of human possibilities, but rather a creation that comes from God: as strange, astonishing, and unpredictable as the first creation.

When we have recentered everything on the person of Jesus Christ and made everything start with Him, as the entire New Testament does, we cannot follow Garaudy's reasoning (which is the same one apologetics always uses). Herein lies Garaudy's significance: in spite of his having become a Christian, he cannot forgo the method logically started off by a *rational* approach (not necessarily Marxist); all who subscribe to this brand of Marxism inevitably use such an argument. It takes as its starting point characteristics common to all people, adding perhaps a tiny dose of Christianity, which is not really even necessary. Considering how far he has already come, I feel sure Garaudy will finally place Jesus Christ in the center and ascribe to Him the same fulness we see in Paul's writings. The path followed by Marxist Christians, however, is exactly the opposite: Jesus, charged with a historical revolutionary mission, becomes an insignificant, pale shadow, because this role has exhausted all the fulness of His truth.

Amazingly (in a January 1979 statement), Jean Ellenstein comes to the same conclusion as Garaudy. He opens up the possibility of a future conciliation of Marxism and Christianity. Ellenstein forcefully affirms the impossibility of any attempt to synthesize Christianity and Communism ("Any attempt to produce a Christian Marxism is doomed to failure"), and I am glad for that. He also accepts that as a Marxist one can no longer deny that faith is an irrepressible dimension of the human spirit. But, like Garaudy, Ellenstein uses "faith" to mean "faith in itself." After these statements, Ellenstein arrives at an extremely hackneyed conclusion: we must simply separate the two spheres. Faith must remain a private expression, an aspect of the personal spiritual life; Christianity must renounce politics. Marxism must cease to lean on philosophical materialism and move on to a political phase of maturity. Thus a person can be a believer as far as faith and transcendence are concerned, and at the same time a Marxist with respect to his concept of history and his methodology of political and social action. We have been hearing this for a long time: faith is a strictly private, inner matter, and you are free to *believe* whatever you like, as long as in practice you apply Marxism's directives. In other words, Christian faith must have no ethical or political effect; it belongs in heaven. Marxism deals with practical and concrete issues.

The above leads to the conclusion of these "marginal notes." We have discovered three hypothetical solutions to the problem of reconciling Christian faith and Marxism: synthesis (which Ellenstein finds impossible), the separation of spheres (but Christianity would then be reduced to the spiritual realm and forced to abandon any ethics or specific political action), and the conviction that Christianity as the practice of faith leads to the adoption of Marxism as Christian praxis. The last possibility seems to me to represent the tendency of present-day Marxist Christians. I personally prefer to hold to the radical contradiction between the two, but see them as set in a framework of dialectical conflict, rather than engaged in a mortal conflict destined to eliminate one or the other.

Chapter IV

Service Theology: A Sample Text

Matthew 9:2-13

We have nothing to gain by mounting a heavy biblical or theological offensive against Marxist Christians. Such an apologetic has no rhyme or reason. Nor should we demonstrate, citing chapter and verse, how Marxist Christians have erred biblically. That would fail to convince any of them, and would scarcely help anyone else.

These days we hear broad statements about Jesus' political role, coming principally from the Marxist-Christian world. Some offer us impressive outlines of Jesus' political position (Jean Cardonnel's *Un trafic d'armes*, for example), or allusions to biblical texts that they carefully avoid examining closely. These "theologians" consider anyone who takes a biblical text in its entirety and listens to it a petty bourgeois intellectual. Such a biblical stance, they feel, shows that a person is unaware of his alienation and has not realized that the correct, materialist approach to a biblical text does not get bogged down in its literal meaning.

I am going to risk such criticism by discussing a passage from the Gospel of Matthew (9:2-13), because it is often alluded to for the purpose of justifying the theological positions mentioned above. We will put verse 9, concerning the call of Matthew, in parentheses, since it forms the transition to the scene where Jesus eats at a tax collector's house. The result is a coherent text: Jesus, scandalizing the theologians, forgives the sins of a paralytic and then heals him. He "merely" renders a service: He responds "medically" to a man's human expectation, without preaching to him. Hence this passage provides a basis for the theology of service. In response to Jesus' act, the crowd glorifies God, "who had given such authority to men" (v. 8).

Thus, we are told, Jesus is not an inimitable, exceptional man; on the contrary, the passage invites us to do the same thing, acting like this man, Jesus, who has only human power.

The second half of the text shows Jesus eating with tax collectors and "sinners," and criticized for it by moralists and respectable people. Jesus answers that the sick people are those who need a physician, and quotes the Bible: "learn what this means: 'I desire mercy, and not sacrifice'" (v. 13). One could easily draw the conclusion that offering sacrifices and burnt offerings to God has no value, nor would worship, which has taken the place of sacrifice in our day. Such "service" to God is apparently useless. True service to God means serving humanity, and the proper context for such service is not worship but the practice of mercy and compassion: action on behalf of the poorest of the poor, the disinherited. We must suffer with those who suffer, help them, and accompany them along the way; this is God's will *in its entirety.*

Jesus would appear, then, in these two scenes, to set aside worship, discourse, and morality (He rejects the moral people: they have no need of a physician). We hear His words all over again: "Not everyone who says to me 'Lord, Lord,' shall enter the kingdom of heaven" (7:21). We see in this passage what the new vocabulary calls an example of Jesus' "practice": He *heals* from sickness, He *forgives.* Does He forgive sins? We define *sin,* according to the new theologians, as follows: social ostracism that makes the paralytic not only a sick person but someone unworthy of entering God's service. We know, for example, that the Essenes excluded the infirm, and paralytics expressly, from their community. In addition, by His presence among tax collectors and prostitutes, Jesus *rehabilitates,* on the social and political level, those who are excluded: rejected and despised people. This is mercy. In these two scenes we do not see God, or obedience to the law, or a mystical or spiritual overevaluation of Jesus' action.

This first reading of the passage appears amply reinforced by the two following comments. First, when the crowd sees the healing miracle, they glorify God! This clearly shows talk is unnecessary! Jesus did not need to preach about God, or even to say He was acting in God's name. The crowd understands in-

stinctively, without intermediary, so that the witness to God is
accomplished without words or preaching. The service Jesus
renders suffices in itself. Thus the "theology of service" seems
fully justified: when true service takes place, it turns people to
God much more surely than any words can do. Religious discourse unaccompanied by acts confirming it have been the
surest way to turn people away from the Church. The same text
recalling that this power has been given to human beings seems
to justify "horizontal theology," since the necessary thing is a
human *action* rather than a prayer causing God to act directly.
Jesus does not speak to God: He speaks on His own to the paralytic. People possess all the powers and characteristics needed
to exercise mercy.

The second comment is also basic: Jesus, in the presence of
tax collectors and prostitutes, does nothing. Clearly He fails to
pronounce, in their midst as well, any discourse—whether religious (concerning God), or political (in which He would explain to these people that they have dignity in spite of their social status). Jesus does nothing, says nothing, except perhaps for
insignificant remarks during a meal. He limits Himself to *being*
with them, in their midst. He eats with them, and thus allows
Himself to be served. He does not put these people on a pedestal
by serving them.

But Jesus does not give them a moral lesson, either. Concretely, He does not call them to repentance (we must see clearly
that they were truly loose-living people; in spite of modern ra-
tionalizations, prostitution cannot be equated with sainthood in
God's sight; and tax collectors were given to theft and attempted
to exploit people under their authority). Thus Jesus' mere presence rehabilitates these people, so that they are no longer pari-
ahs.

Logically, then, it is enough for us to "be *with*": with the
poor, to accomplish God's will. Mercy means being with them,
in their midst, rehabilitating them so they can be something
other than despised. But since such rehabilitation constitutes a
break with social custom, it is also a political matter. We must
never preach to such people or try to proselytize them, according to service theology. Being with them suffices; in order to be
reestablished in their human dignity, they need not come to

faith in Jesus Christ. Thus the meaning of this passage seems obvious.

1. Sin and Preaching

Such comments on the passage go too far, however. At least one word should draw our attention toward another dimension of the text: sin. "Your sins are forgiven" (Matt. 9:2) ; "I came . . . to call . . . sinners" (v. 13). We must dismiss at the outset an objection that often surfaces these days because of cultural relativism in sociology. Someone says "the use of the word *sin* is unimportant. Jesus merely adopts the vocabulary common to His time. He says 'sin' because people understood what the word meant. Otherwise. . . ." But if "sin" does not mean "sin," what did Jesus mean by the word? What was He naming when He used this word that was culturally understood?

The paralytic needs *forgiveness*. We must not be dishonest at this point and try to transpose this term onto a sociopolitical plane. Jesus calls the others "sick," after all (v. 12). These people do not just have the reputation of being ill: they *are* ill. Tax collectors *are* thieves and exploiters of the poor. They harm others. The issue is not only social and moral. These people are not judged just by others to be sinners: Jesus also has no doubt they are sinners.

He does not say to the paralytic or to the prostitutes that they have every reason to be what they are, that He accepts their actions, etc. No: to the paralytic He announces forgiveness (which he truly *needs*, so that we can perfectly well use the term *sin!*); to the others Jesus declares He is the physician and the one who calls. And in Israel, after all, call and vocation had a definite spiritual meaning. "Sin" is not an ordinary word Jesus uses for convenience' sake. The Bible strictly defines the term, and nothing would authorize us to claim that in this context Jesus deviates from biblical usage, since He takes the position of God, who forgives sins. In no way does Jesus transpose sin onto the sociopolitical realm. He simply declares that *He* forgives sin in *all* its dimensions (including the political and social).

In the Bible, sin always relates necessarily to God. No merely human sin, against another person, exists: "Against thee, thee only, have I sinned" (Ps. 51:4). In other words, Jesus has not "rendered service" here at all; He has not primarily healed, for example. The text emphasizes clearly forgiveness of sins and not healing: healing comes only as a kind of proof ad absurdum that Jesus can forgive sins. So forgiveness of sins is the central theme of the passage.

How does this theme relate to the objection to sacrifices that follows it? Clearly, sacrifices and burnt offerings (not all, but many of them) are instituted for forgiveness of sins, purification, and absolution—so that an individual or a people can be restored to innocence. Thus the message of this passage has nothing to do with the fraudulent interpretation that service theology tries to give it: that is, that "sermons and worship are pointless, since true worship is service." On the contrary, the point is that since Jesus forgives sins, sacrifices for the purpose of absolution have become useless and should be abolished. Jesus has become the scapegoat for all time; He is the absolute sacrifice. Thus He devaluates all others. This passage takes its place as a significant aspect of the theology of salvation rather than belonging to a theology of service or of politics.

Furthermore, we must answer the criticism that the service Jesus renders is sufficient in itself, since people glorify *God* even though Jesus has not mentioned Him! Such an interpretation cannot be taken seriously. We must, after all, remember the context in which Jesus acts. Rather than a context of class struggle, we have here a people steeped in the Word of God, who normally and spontaneously relate everything to God, even when they are disobedient, and in whose view God acts continually. A person belonging to this people has been formed by generations, each of which has contributed its interpretation of how things relate to God. In this context, a person never errs when something amazing or wonderful happens: he knows whom to glorify, and spontaneously he turns toward God.

Jesus need not make a speech to explain that He acts in God's name. He need not give any teaching; it would merely repeat what these people know perfectly well. In fact, as many have noted, Jesus' teaching concerning the "Old" Testament is not really *new*: the new element is that the Word has become flesh, so that everything that was *said* is now *lived*. Prophecies are now fulfilled.

These fulfillments, these things that are now lived, and this "service" have meaning and bring light only because of what was proclaimed and incorporated into people's consciousness. So Jesus' failure to preach here offers no example for us, since we live in a society that is precisely the opposite of the one in which He lived. Today people relate nothing to God, and have no knowledge of God's Word in Jesus Christ. Consequently the proclamation and designation of Jesus Christ, and His teaching and preaching, form the main, indispensable element in this passage. His service comes next and is practically secondary. Naturally, *we* feel a need to "render service," in order to escape from Jesus' "I never knew you" (Matt. 7:23), and because we must not separate Word and life, but rather live out the declaration of love. But what matters to the other person is that he has turned toward God and the resurrection. This matters much more than having a social problem resolved.

Concerning Jesus' silent presence among tax collectors and prostitutes, people whose lives fail to measure up, we must first note that these people are not poor: tax collectors are *all* wealthy, collaborators of the Romans, and exploiters of the people.[1] The prostitutes are wealthy women of the town. Their "poverty" consists of being misjudged by others—not so much by "proper people" as by Jews hostile to the Roman invaders and Jews faithful to the religion of their fathers. According to these people, tax collectors and prostitutes are sinners, and we have seen that Jesus confirms their judgment. Tax collectors and prostitutes are trapped in a blind alley: since they are no longer faithful to the religion of the God of Abraham, they cannot offer sacrifices for their sin, and are therefore permanently locked up in it.

At this point, in relation to this situation, Jesus proclaims mercy. That is, God forgives sin even when there is no sacrifice, worship, etc.; therefore we also must practice unconditional love, as God does. The issue is not the social "rehabilitation" of these tax collectors, etc., particularly since Jesus does not reha-

---

1. For more detail concerning the tax collectors' position, see Chapter V.

bilitate them. On the contrary, He identifies Himself with them, and causes Himself to be rejected with them. The point of the passage is accomplishing the fulfillment of the Old Testament's proclamation: forgiveness. Any effort at social rehabilitation, re-classification, etc., can only be the expression, the demonstration, or the visible presence of the *accomplished forgiveness of sin.*

Living like Jesus, then, means first of all bringing forgiveness of sin to people in their anguish, uneasiness, exasperation, guilt, self-accusation, despair, withdrawal, and loneliness. We must proclaim this message to all the poor, the excluded, the mis-judged. This passage does not deal with moral types of sin (our text fails to mention forgiveness of sin for the proud, the power-ful, the self-satisfied, the conquerors, and the unscrupulous, but of course they too can receive forgiveness, once they have been led to the discovery of their emptiness). We need to accompany immigrant workers and proletarians not to convert them to some Christian formula, not to serve them and take up their political cause, but to proclaim the forgiveness of their sin: to bear witness to their liberation in Christ. This proclamation must take place well before we take the first step to deliver them politically. I insist this must happen *before,* and not afterward or concurrently! For this is what the text teaches.

2. Mercy and Piety

At the end of our passage Jesus quotes the Old Testament: "Go and learn what this means, 'I desire mercy, and not sacrifice'" (Matt. 9:13). This verse reflects two Old Testament contexts. Lit-erally, the words come from Hosea 6:1-6:

> 1 "Come, let us return to the Lord;
>   for he has torn, that he may heal us;
>   he has stricken, and he will bind us up.
> 2 After two days he will revive us;
>   on the third day he will raise us up,
>   that we may live before him.
> 3 Let us know, let us press on to know the Lord;
>   his going forth is sure as the dawn;
>   he will come to us as the showers,
>   as the spring rains that water the earth."

4 What shall I do with you, O Ephraim?
What shall I do with you, O Judah?
Your love is like a morning cloud,
like the dew that goes early away.
5 Therefore I have hewn them by the prophets,
I have slain them by the words of my mouth,
and my judgment goes forth as the light.
6 For I desire steadfast love and not sacrifice,
the knowledge of God, rather than burnt offerings.

Clearly, however, Jesus' phrase in Matthew 9:13 also recalls Psalm 50, where God proclaims that sacrifices are secondary:

8 "I do not reprove you for your sacrifices;
your burnt offerings are continually before me.

. . . .

14 Offer to God a sacrifice of thanksgiving,
and pay your vows to the Most High;
15 and call upon me in the day of trouble;
I will deliver you, and you shall glorify me."
16 But to the wicked God says:
"What right have you to recite my statutes,
or take my covenant on your lips?"

. . . .

23 "He who brings thanksgiving as his sacrifice honors me."

We must remember that Jesus speaks to people with a thorough knowledge of the Bible, especially in this dispute, where He speaks to Pharisees. Thus, as soon as Jesus cites a single biblical word or phrase, His hearers recognize it, since they have it memorized. Jesus need not quote the whole passage, since whatever phrase He chooses brings with it, for His hearers, all the rest. Consequently, if we wish to understand Jesus' words and actions, we must place ourselves within this frame of reference and hear His words in their whole context. Rather than putting on scholarly airs, by this effort we simply try to hear Jesus' words as His hearers heard them!

If we take the passage from Hosea, we find love and knowledge of God opposed expressly to sacrifices and burnt offerings, which most certainly include ritual, liturgy, morality, the commandments, and, of course, the organization of the Church. Jesus calls this love and knowledge of God "mercy." In so doing, He does not annul the text of Hosea; rather, He clarifies the text through this interpretation, and in turn He clarifies the meaning of mercy through the text of Hosea. Love, not sacrifice, is central—love which expresses itself in these manifestations of adoration for God.

When Jesus quotes the Hosea passage, then, He by no means does away with its orientation toward God. Jesus does not say "Do away with sacrifices (because they are oriented toward God) and practice mercy (because it expresses love of neighbor)." Mercy and piety are identified with each other. So love of neighbor is not to be substituted for love of God, since it is *in second place*, though *similar*. We are to practice mercy in order to have true piety rather than just formal piety.

Here we have, then, a call to earnestness. We must be serious about worshiping God. Hosea teaches that ritual, habitual temple attendance, leading a life in keeping with the Law—all this has no value if our worship is not *lived*, if our faith is not intimate, personal, and profound. Our faith must be turned toward God. All our actions have meaning and value through faith. But since this God we worship is Love, since love is the first commandment, how could we exclude the person who needs to be loved? Clearly we must love him, manifesting our love as concretely as possible, in every area—including political and social. Mercy takes place in love and piety. When Jesus finds Himself in a situation where piety needs to express itself in love of neighbor, He transforms piety into mercy. He does this not in some definitive manner that would produce a permanent substitution, but in the here-and-now situation of His relationship with the Pharisees, in order to show them how to interpret the Hosea passage in their present situation.

This conclusion suggests the second parallel, also in Hosea: "the knowledge of God rather than burnt offerings" (Hos. 6:6; we must immediately clarify and caution: knowing God means *seeking* to know God, as in v. 3: "Let us know, let us press on to know the Lord"). Thus, associated with mercy we have everything related to reading the Scriptures, openness to the mystery of revelation, etc. Of course we should engage in Bible study and preaching! When He refers to the Hosea passage, Jesus includes all of this. But precisely because of His reference to Hosea, Jesus cannot mean formal, metaphysical, ritually based knowledge.

What God does Hosea refer to when he enjoins: "Let us press on to know the Lord" (6:3)? He tears, but heals us, gives life and raises us up (vv. 1-2); His promises are absolutely reliable, and He never lies: the God who delivers and liberates, the utterly faithful God. In other words, Hosea's hearers must learn of the living God (rather than the motionless God to whom they offered sacrifices), the God who acts and intervenes (rather than the God of ritual and liturgies), the God of history (rather than the God of ceremonies).

"What shall I do with you, O Ephraim? What shall I do with you, O Judah?" (v. 4). We can have complete confidence in this God who changes everything. Our hope exists because He is coming. In other words, the passage in Hosea sets up a contrast between purely formal religious practice and the conviction that everything comes from God; between acts that can be repeated indefinitely and the intervention of the Lord. Therefore, in order to have some understanding of what worship and sacrifice entail, one must first know *this* God.

And just when Hosea's words are forcibly recalled to the memory of Jesus' hearers, those words are fulfilled, because He is there. This is the God Jesus makes known by His ministry and His whole being. When Jesus approaches sinners, He brings with Him *this* knowledge of God. By practicing mercy, Jesus shows what it means to know God. This knowledge cannot exist apart from mercy. But knowledge is not vain or negligible: everything is bound up together: Hosea's prophecy is fulfilled but nothing is set aside. So mercy does not take the place of everything else; rather, we see the fulfillment and the realization of the promise.

We can now consider the text from Psalm 50. The writer opposes verbal goodness (v. 16: "What right have you to recite my statutes, or take my covenant on your lips?"), accompanied by worship and sacrifices, to two other attitudes before God: thanksgiving (v. 14) and calling upon Him (v. 15). Here again, therefore, we have a text to which Jesus alludes but which *directs everything toward God rather than toward humanity.* Even when we are wretched, we must thank God: "Offer to God a sacrifice of thanksgiving" (v. 14). At all times, our heart, in gratitude springing from our whole being, should engage in this thanksgiving that takes the place of ceremony and formalism.

To be sure, mercy is an expression of thanksgiving; the person committed to God shows through the person committed to others. But thanksgiving comes first and forms the foundation. Thanksgiving when we are unhappy, because God remains with us in spite of everything (and in Jesus Christ He shares our wretchedness). The mercy that moves us to share the suffering of others cannot, in a revolt brought on by injustice or poverty, drown out this thanksgiving. It persists in spite of the suffering in which we are submerged.

Right after the psalmist's call to thanksgiving he calls us to its counterpart: "Call upon me in the day of trouble; I will deliver you, and you shall glorify me" (v. 15). In other words, from our distress we must first call to God, rather than first calling for human help or giving it. This invocation, made in absolute confidence and certainty, is the most decisive factor. It replaces sacrifice, when sacrifice is conceived as a kind of bargain: I give something to God so He will then give me something; I sacrifice in order to have a claim on God. But this passage proclaims the contrary: absolute gratuitousness. Calling on God suffices.

Yet we have all had many times the experience of God's failure to deliver or answer us. Is grace so reliable? What can we say about the growth of poverty and injustice in Christendom? Precisely against these facts our faith and hope must rise up. What would faith mean if we saw clearly what God is doing? What would hope mean if God suddenly, like a vending machine, performed everything we asked of Him? Would He be God then?

In short, the psalmist, like Hosea, questions ecclesiastical, cultural, moral, and legalistic patterns. But not for the purpose of turning us to a theology of service, an exclusively horizontal relationship in which human beings serve others. On the contrary, the psalmist wants to lead us to take God utterly seriously first: God to the exclusion of human means and *human systems.*

For cultural and sacrificial patterns were just that: human techniques for obtaining certain results. Such techniques are excluded by the author, who refers to the grace of God *alone;* beginning with that grace, human action on behalf of others will be possible, but only beginning there, not based on any other point of departure, foundation, relationship, or understanding of the situation.

The psalmist tells us that we must internalize our relationship with God. We must personalize it and integrate it with our whole being, through continual thanksgiving and calling on God. Only afterward, as a consequence, does service of our neighbor become truly possible. With Hosea and the psalmist, then, we return to our basic assertion: no love, mercy, or compassion for others can exist unless we first practice piety, prayer, and thanksgiving.

Jesus' listeners inevitably and spontaneously understood this assertion as the overtone and connotation of Jesus' declaration: "I desire mercy, and not sacrifice" (Matt. 9:13). These simple words inevitably evoked the images and comments from Hosea and Psalm 50, to which the passage in Matthew alludes briefly when it states: "the crowds . . . glorified God" (Matt. 9:8). *We have no coincidence here: these words repeat the psalmist's* "Call upon me in the day of trouble; I will deliver you, and you shall glorify me" (Ps. 50:15). Jesus calls on God (He was not simply a miracle worker!); the paralytic is delivered; the crowd glorifies God. The passage that follows clearly relates to this glorification, so that the two parts of the passage go together.

You may object, however, that Jesus has changed something; rather than finding Hosea and the psalmist sufficient in their substitution of piety for ritual, Jesus goes a step further. Instead of speaking of "piety, thanksgiving, calling on God, and knowing Him," Jesus has transposed all these into mercy; that is, Jesus takes something directed toward God in the Old Testament and brings it down to earth (since mercy is directed only toward people, in a purely human context), considering only human beings. We will see that this is a "materialist" exegesis. But it has no adequate basis.

Jesus substitutes neither His authority nor His word for Scripture. We cannot get away from His statements: "Think not that I have come to abolish the law and the prophets; I have come not to abolish them but to fulfil them. . . . Not an iota, not a dot, will pass from the law" (Matt. 5:17-18). Jesus indicates the meaning of Hosea's prophecy and of the psalm; He carries them out and gives them their fulness, but does not eliminate His relationship with His Father. Mercy is first of all God's mercy; as Jesus moves the emphasis toward humanity, He takes another step along the path of truth, but this in no way constitutes a substitution or an abrogation of what had been proclaimed.

3. Presuppositions and Interpretation

Thus when we compare Matthew 9 with the Old Testament texts Jesus refers to we understand how illegitimate it is to use His words to construct a horizontal theology of service. This discovery prompts us to ask, as many others have done, about the proper assumptions for understanding a biblical text. Certainly the reader may label my interpretation "classical," "theological," "bourgeois," etc. For these days everyone agrees we inevitably read a text through our own "grid," by means of our culture's images and concepts, our prejudices, and, if one is Marxist, through our class affiliation.

This concept has two aspects: (1) All reading is purely subjective (I understand on the basis of *my* training, *my* culture, etc., and never attain any objective meaning); objectivity remains permanently unattainable. (2) All reading is necessarily biased. My self-interest leads me to read so that my situation is reinforced. In the extreme point of view, my self-interest determines my understanding, so that my only intent is justifying my condition (that is, my "class condition").

Those who formulated these two principles believed they were making considerable strides toward truth, displaying great honesty and genuine humility. Whereas actually, as so often happens, though their point of departure was quite correct, they drifted from it toward a series of wild assertions. Their correct point of departure involves two principles. First, obviously, we can read and understand a text only with the accumulation of ideas and values we possess. Some subjectivity, then, is essential; without it the text would remain dead. The difference in cultures obliges us to reread the text in a new way and to bring it to life again.

A second correct principle underlying erroneous ideas about subjective and biased interpretation has to do with experimentation: we can, of course, attempt to read a text in order to justify ourselves and to show we are right. But this approach has no necessary connection with our class identification. Often individuals read a biblical passage to find in it the confirmation of what they are or what they want to do. Jesus' condemnation of the Pharisees relates to this kind of bias (the Pharisees were by no means "bourgeois" as far as their financial means were concerned). We can go further: certainly the nineteenth-century Protestant bourgeoisie also read the Bible in order to feel collectively justified in its endeavors and to show the legitimacy of its domination as a class.

Such a practice is neither universal nor permanent. Since it exists, however, scholars have leaped from there to amazing conclusions. First, let's look at cultural subjectivity. Certainly we see and understand everything through the tinted glasses given us by our society, our culture. But we must remember the other side of the coin: thanks to these glasses we can enter into a relationship with others. If I claim to reach by myself an objective truth or reality outside the values and interpretations of my society, I cut myself off completely from other people (furthermore, mercy becomes impossible!).

We hear constantly proclaimed these days that the language we teach children is oppressive, repressive, a ready-made cage designed to mold their spirit and to eliminate their freedom. How absurd! Such foolish thinking ignores the fact that without this language, a child could not communicate with anyone; instead of being free, he would simply be an idiot (in both the etymological and current meanings of the word!). This "repression" amounts to the necessary condition of "being with others" and having the possibility of communicating with them.

Acculturation, criticized for limiting us to subjective understanding, turns out to be at the same time the necessary condition for objectivity. What is objectivity, after all, if not general agreement on a given meaning, value, or interpretation? Without this common consent, all we have left is raving and drifting. We must of course take into account that "general agreement" is not total agreement and that considerable margin and a certain play in language always exist.

In short, what meaning can we find in all this pessimistic talk about the "grid" imposed on us? It means only that we never reach the object itself; our cultural glasses act as a filter between us and the object. In other words, all the talk boils down to a platitude: we never know reality in itself, we never reach absolute truth. Nothing deeper can be found in these pompous assertions reverberating among the wise thinkers of our time. It may be useful, however, to emphasize the leap involved in this thinking, since it occurs often: since all knowledge and interpretation take place through a filter, so that no absolutely objective knowledge can be had, we may indulge in anything! Whether we say one thing or the other makes no difference, since in any case it is not the "Truth."

At this point we arrive at hypocrisy. For even if absolute objectivity is impossible, a degree of objectivity can be attained by applying a rigorous method of inquiry (but I know that this method itself is bound up with a given cultural tendency and milieu). We can reach even greater objectivity by comparing our findings with other times, cultures, and interpretations. I need to admit that I, and those like me, do not begin at the beginning. Especially in the case of a biblical text, it is essential, in view of my cultural limitations, to listen to the interpretations coming from other milieux and cultures, and to be confronted with all the past—all the periods of church history. Because for each period a different understanding of the text has rung true.

This approach does not amount to relativism. It in no way prevents me from having my present-day interpretation; it simply forbids me to say that the Church until now has always come up with erroneous interpretations, and that we have at last arrived at a correct understanding (so that we continually discover what Jesus meant!). Nevertheless, I am obliged to say, "I firmly believe my understanding to be the *useful* interpretation for people and society today, given the present circumstances."

We must go on, however, to the claim that "class interpretation" is inevitable. One thing leads to another. Where do the "glasses" through which we read everything come from? Surely those who believe the glasses come from society or culture in general, from the ideas of an epoch, are mistaken! No—since Marx we have known that "the prevailing ideas come from the ruling class."[2] Therefore, our a prioris, our reading "grids," and the stereotypes we use to interpret are all produced by the ruling class. Consequently, the ruling class of one period of history produces a text and then the ruling class of another period reads and understands it (this reasoning assumes that everyone agrees that there are "classes" in all societies; we will return to this matter in Chapter V). In this view, the only possible reading and understanding of a text are based on class.

Before we even look at a text, then, according to these experts, we must ask which social class produced it (thus the famous, apparently innocuous question, "Where are you speaking from?"). I can understand the intention of a text only in relation to its class-interest objective. In the extreme view, the only content of any text amounts to class defense. So what a text says holds no interest for us, since we *must* understand it as situated within the class struggle, as having the purpose of intellectually repressing the dominated class.

If the only possible interpretation involves a subconscious class interpretation, however, I must be honest enough to declare that I *must* interpret this way. Since I cannot escape such an interpretation, I can at least do it consciously! Then things will be clear and aboveboard. Especially since if I submit to the unconscious influence, I will inevitably interpret from the point of view of the ruling class; whereas if I decide to make a class interpretation, I obviously have a choice! This way I can interpret the text according to the dominated class's perspective and

---

2. Althusser brilliantly transformed this idea into the celebrated ISA, the Ideological State Apparatus, and intellectuals ate it up. The notion makes no new contribution, except for its name! Furthermore, this idea of Marx's contradicts what I showed above: that the dominant ideology of the Western world today is socialism. To understand how we got to this point, the reader should consult my *Métamorphose du bourgeois* (Paris: Calmann-Lévy, 1967), in which I show how the bourgeoisie had no difficulty integrating socialism and Marxism all the while remaining basically true to itself.

in terms of its interests.[3] If, therefore, I side with the poor and oppressed, I *must* do a class-oriented interpretation; I must choose to interpret and manipulate the text in accordance with the struggle of the downtrodden class. Q.E.D. All Marxist-Christian exegesis and theology rest on this reasoning. Let us take a closer look at it.

If we wish to analyze how such interpretation works, we must distinguish two levels: on the first level, we recognize that our society and culture impose a certain interpretation of things on us. This imposition applies to everything, including scientific research and the most objective scientific thought. But our "grid" of interpretation acts effectively, inevitably, and irreparably only when we are completely unconscious and ignorant of it. The grid must be so much a part of me and so closely entwined with my whole personality that I cannot even begin to notice it.

Only when I fail to realize that I have colored glasses am I absolutely convinced things are colored a certain way. If I begin to reflect and remind myself that I wear glasses, I realize they may distort what objects I see. If my glasses are tinted, they give things a different hue. At that point, I question what I thought was absolutely correct, objective, and unchallengeable. As soon as I make this suspicion my own, presuppositions and stereotypes stop playing their role. Only in the case of utter ignorance of the filter of cultural understanding, through which I see and read everything, can we speak of bias, since my ignorance leads me to believe I have reached the object itself.

I can criticize all sorts of presuppositions, but then they *no longer influence me.* Once I can see them in this light, their role

---

3. Such reasoning confronts us with a mystery as impenetrable as creation *ex nihilo!* If the prevailing ideas are truly those of the ruling class, if all ideological process depends on the reproduction of this domination, if the Ideological State Apparatus is inevitable, how could the dominated class come up with any specific, autonomous, independent ideas? Either the dominated class has a capacity for original thought, in which case it is not genuinely alienated, or else it is totally dominated, and no understanding based on its ideas is possible. Bakunin wondered where Marx's own thought came from, in view of these considerations, and Marx could never find an answer!

has been reduced to an appearance, something mythological (not mythical!). Once I can designate the mystifier, it no longer has any power over me, but I become beholden to another one that goes undetected. My cultural milieu continually provides new filters; each time I unconsciously receive a new one, I become able to designate and expose my previous, distorted way of looking at things. I will give two examples without elaborating on them.

Marx eagerly pursued these presuppositions, the distorted and distorting ideas of the ruling class with its bad conscience. His system *as a whole*, however, in both its philosophical and economic aspects, and his concept of history, depend on two ideas he never makes explicit and never criticizes: work and progress.

For Marx, work is the key to everything: human specificity, the means of becoming human, the source of value, the possibility of creating added value, the condition of history, the basis of the relationship between an individual and the rest of humanity, the uniting factor of the species, etc. In reality this idea appears in the seventeenth century as a very specific bourgeois ideology. It is a typical ruling-class ideology, since work considered as the supreme human value enables the ruling class to justify its domination as the class requiring others to work. Marx's distinction between alienated labor and emancipated labor changes nothing here; on the contrary, it merely repeats a cherished idea of the eighteenth-century bourgeoisie. Marx understood everything through this filter; yet if you remove the concept of work from Marx's system, you are left with *nothing*.

Marx's other unexamined presupposition is progress. His dialectic is a dialectic of progress. Each stage rises higher than the preceding one: each period of history progresses with respect to the preceding period. Humanity progresses constantly. Marx's vision as determined by the idea of progress leads him to conceive of the flow of human prehistory into history, and the consummation of class struggle in socialism. We can consider socialism, as both human achievement and nearly inevitable result of the course of history, as certain only because of the ideology of progress.

On the basis of this "pre-interpretation" of history, scholars try to assure us that Marx established a scientific method and provided us with a veritable science of society, history, etc. But this science depends on an unexamined ideology. Furthermore, this ideology of progress, utterly unsubstantiated, turns out to be a product of eighteenth-century bourgeois thinking. Marx is a bourgeois thinker. He never got out from under the substructures of bourgeois thinking, because he never noticed them. He never realized that everything rested on flimsy presuppositions. We cannot simply say, "Of course Marx is not timeless; he shared the ideas of his time." We must admit that since he failed to criticize his presuppositions and built everything on them, we cannot consider his system more scientific than others. Nor can we consider class struggle, for example, as an absolute, objective truth that clarifies all of history!

Our second example, while less weighty, dates from more recent times: citing Psalm 8, Christians and theologians objected to my efforts to explain technique between 1950 and 1960. They found my analysis pessimistic, coming at a time when euphoria dominated, because of current scientific, technical, and economic expansion. People were convinced by notions of unlimited progress, technique's beneficent nature, complete human mastery of technique and therefore of the world. All difficulties would soon be resolved. In the midst of this angelic agreement, I came across as a backward imbecile, an unconscious wet blanket.

So they read Psalm 8 as a justification for the technological conquest, the passage providing the theological undergirding of this great human enterprise. In vain I tried to show that the text said exactly the opposite ("*Thou* [God] hast put all things under his [human] feet" [v. 6]; *God* put creation under humanity's feet, whereas humanity takes possession of it, through technique!). My words had no effect; the text vanished because of the colored glasses of interpretation prescribed by the exhilaration over our society's development. Our friends the theologians knew nothing about the glasses.

Since about 1966, when a period of unrest began, no one has called Psalm 8 to my attention. The colored glasses have been broken. This anecdote shows that only when influenced by an unknown, unconscious filter of interpretation can people obliterate or radically change a text or the facts. The minute they detect the filter as a filter, they can expose it, so that it no longer acts as a filter. It no longer has any role to play.[4]

Up to this point we have spoken only about the first level of analysis of subjective interpretation. On the second level, a person deals with the problem of subjectivity by saying: "Since historical objectivity is impossible, I can say anything at all; since I inevitably interpret through a 'grid,' I might as well choose one at random" (instead of trying to detect and criticize the grids imposed on me). "Since I cannot escape making a class interpretation, I will do it with gusto. And since the dreadful bourgeois lies as he makes his bourgeois interpretation, I will interpret from the proletarian point of view. The proletarian interpretation is just as false, but its falsification lies on the proper side."

---

4. Have we absolutely no way to escape such a limited interpretation? Can we detect our reading filters and thus render them obsolete only after the passage of time and sociological change? Will we never have a true understanding of the biblical text, for example? This question has fundamental importance. On the one hand, we never escape our historical context and will never reach the unique, absolute interpretation. But on the other hand, we have the possibility of detecting our current cultural "glasses" and of access to a *truthful* understanding of the text. This is available to us not through a good scientific method, but—and I apologize for reverting to this apparently glib cliché—through the Holy Spirit. Only the Holy Spirit can enable us to reach an understanding of the text *different* from the sociological and class understanding. The interpretation arrived at through the Holy Spirit corresponds to God's eternal will as well as His will in the present. Only the Holy Spirit can accomplish this, because He is independent of historical circumstances, and because He is the Spirit of light.

You find this glib and simplistic? Try it and see for yourself! That is my only suggestion. You find it easy to free yourself from your cherished "personal" ideas because the Holy Spirit compels you to? Easy to submit yourself to the free operation of this Spirit you are never sure will be given to you for even a moment? Only those who have no idea what is involved could be so foolish as to call it easy. I repeat that only the Holy Spirit can make the text *speak*, because only God can speak rightly of God. There is nothing beyond Him. All the talk about sociological "grids" of understanding falls far short. As I have shown in another connection, only the concept of a Transcendent One can enable us to comprehend the data of a world organized like ours.

When people suggest "interpretation from within class struggle," they are actually proposing apologetic interpretation: interpretation falsified for a good cause. On the first level, as we have shown, involuntary, unconscious falsification takes place. But on this second level, we are dealing with lying. For class interpretation fails utterly to reestablish the truth of the text; rather it involves interpreting for the benefit of those whose side we have taken. We could compare the use of propaganda for the purpose of fighting propaganda, which never tends toward a return to accurate information!

Taking a position in this class interpretation, then, means getting embroiled in a maze of contradictions and relying on untenable presuppositions. You question whether untenable presuppositions are involved? How about: "The text has no meaning; it receives its meaning only when situated externally. We must place the text outside itself, in the situation of class struggle, which precedes it." This thinking leads to a confused mass of contradictions: the text necessarily emanates from the ruling classes, and expresses their thought; it is situated within the class struggle. But according to our presupposition, we must interpret the text on the basis of the ideology of the dominated class: that is, we must interpret it in a manner that contradicts it. In other words, we superimpose on the text something it cannot have meant, but which means a great deal to us. We return to the well-known methods of apologetics and the Delphinian use of a poor, innocent text!

Each time we *use* the biblical text *in order to* prove we are right in having adopted a given theological or political option, we involve ourselves in untruth—untruth in the theological sense, coming from the kingdom of the Prince of lies. Again, this is the only result of materialist exegesis based on class struggle.

Chapter V

A Materialist Reading
of the Gospels*

1. Preliminary Considerations and Points of Agreement

Obviously we cannot speak in the abstract about the materialist reading of the Gospels; we can do so only on the basis of the work done by those who claim they have accomplished such a reading. For this reason in the following pages I will attempt to evaluate this work without going into general methodological discussions. I will refer primarily to Fernando Belo's book, since Michel Clévenot's is only a résumé, a simplification that adds practically nothing.[1]

---

* Originally published as "Sur une lecture matérialiste des Evangiles," *Foi et Vie*, 75, nos. 5-6 (Dec. 1976) 20-47. Partial translation by José-María Blanch published as "Concerning a Materialist Reading of the Gospels," in *Occasional Essays* (San José, Costa Rica), 8, nos. 1-2 (Dec. 1981), 33-44. A fresh translation is offered here.—TRANS.

1. Fernando Belo, *A Materialist Reading of the Gospel of Mark*, trans. Matthew J. O'Connell (Maryknoll, NY: Orbis, 1981; French ed. 1974); Michel Clévenot, *Materialist Approaches to the Bible*, trans. William Nottingham (Maryknoll, NY: Orbis, 1985; French ed. 1976). We can add to these Georges Casalis's chapter on materialist interpretation in his *Correct Ideas Don't Fall from the Skies: Elements for an Inductive Theology*, trans. Sister Jeanne Marie Lyons and Michael John (Maryknoll, NY: Orbis, 1984; French ed. 1977). Belo's book organizes the subject in four parts: Part I, The Concept of "Mode of Production" (An Essay in Formal Theory), in which he establishes his interpretation of the mode of production, its forms and applications. Part II deals with Israel, in two chapters: (1) The Symbolic Order of Ancient Israel (the principal concepts and their relationship to the social order); (2) Palestine in the First Century A.D. (a descriptive picture of the cultural milieu of Jesus and Mark's Gospel). Part III, A Reading of Mark (and a materialist explanation of this Gospel, divided into sequences). Finally, Part IV, An Essay in Materialist Ecclesi-

Belo has his reasons for choosing to be Communist, and perhaps Marxist and revolutionary (in the Marxist sense). He suggests his personal reasons, which clearly merit our respect, in
the various dedications at the beginning of his book. He has
made a political choice, which we do not question. In his book,
however, he does not give us a political study or a socioeconomic and political analysis, or even the results of his research in revolutionary strategy. He presents a study of a biblical text, of which he attempts a political analysis. This kind of
study seems perfectly legitimate to me; contrary to the claims of
some, such analysis is common. Belo presents a Leftist political
analysis, which also seems perfectly normal to me: everyone has
his own grill for interpretation. This grill depends on our ideology,[2] our milieu, and our inevitable cultural stereotypes.

At this point, however, Belo's book begins to disturb: he
maintains that he follows no ideology. Everybody interprets the
Gospel ideologically except him. He produces a scientific reading: the first and only such interpretation. I find this claim utterly unacceptable. Belo's triumphalist attitude pervades his
work; it is as if he says, "Until now, for the last two thousand
years, everyone has covered over the text and falsified Jesus; as
the only scientific interpretation, the materialist approach restores the real Jesus to us." At my age you become rather cyni-

---

ology, including the elaboration of a practice and the criticism of theology as discourse springing from powerlessness and as expression of the
dominant classes' ideology.

2. In the area of scriptural interpretation we are clearly faced with
ideological choices. According to contemporary hermeneutical specialists, there are only three exegetical methods: (1) historical-critical (the
venerable method); (2) structuralist, and now (3) Marxist (concerning
this last method, I have tried above to show that it is not scientific and
that in any case it is quite impossible). Specialists eliminate without even
mentioning, for example, christocentric interpretation, brilliantly il-
lustrated by W. Vischer, or symbolic interpretation. These are brushed
aside, because they are not "scientific," as if the others were, in some basic
fashion! Recently we have witnessed the appearance of a new interpretation grill presented by René Girard in *Des choses cachées depuis la fondation
du monde* (Paris: Grassett, 1978), a nonsacrificial interpretation of biblical
texts. Rather than presenting merely another interpretation, Girard gives
us a genuine method. Since it fits no ideological canon, I feel certain it will
never attract notice or be taken into account by biblical scholars.

cal about such proclamations. During the forty years I have been reading books about the Bible, I have run into this kind of talk over twenty times: "the gospel at last, for the first time, restored in all its truth. . . ." In Belo's attitude we recognize the exclusivity and rigidity of Marxist scientism (which owes so little to Marx's thought!). Scientism claims extraordinary ability to find the truth in all realms, and to construct impregnable fortresses.

Before proceeding to a careful criticism of Belo's project and method, however, I would like to indicate at which points I agree with him and where it seems to me he has made a contribution. First of all, to his great credit, he takes a new look at the text and requires that we read it with the greatest possible care. Here lies the special value of the structuralist approach.

Next, using the now classical distinction between narrative and discourse, Belo shows commendably that scholars have traditionally attached more importance to discourse. We must return to narrative, which is the narration of a *practice*. Belo shows rightly that we have often tried to limit our concern to Jesus' words, being obsessed with the effort to establish "authentic sayings," so that the gospel is reduced to a teaching. But Jesus clearly acted, and we must bring His actions to light again. Most of the time His words relate to or are explained by the action (which Belo calls "practice").

Belo also apparently offers us a partially correct interpretation in his contrast between a system of pollution or contagion and a system of debt.[3] This theory sees two major and strictly opposing tendencies in the Old Testament: one centers on the idea of pollution or contagion, related to the sacred, and leads to purification and holiness. It is a religious system, elaborated by the priestly caste, and can be found primarily in Leviticus. The second system centers on the idea of debt, related to forgiveness of debts and gift, and leads to grace. It is a "social" system,

---

3. Concerning this contrast of two themes, pollution and debt, I must underline, as a point of comparison, Girard's much more profound interpretation (in *Des choses cachées depuis la fondation du monde*) with respect to the sacrificial and nonsacrificial reading of biblical texts. But Girard's approach involves no socioeconomic infrastructure that would permit a Marxist interpretation. The sacrificial interpretation springs from more fundamental facts about human beings and society!

elaborated in popular and prophetic circles, and can be found primarily in Deuteronomy. The first system involves a conservative ideology, whereas the second tends to be revolutionary.

Belo has no difficulty showing that Jesus constantly challenged the pollution system and focused everything on the debt system. I find this interpretation appealing, and perhaps partially correct, but its oversimplification runs up against enormous problems in the Old Testament. Deuteronomy is a priestly text for the most part. How could it be "popular"? Conversely, we often find the idea of pollution and purification in the prophets. At times one must divide a verse into two parts to separate Belo's "debt" from "pollution." And how can he declare that the Decalogue is "the summary of the taboos in the debt system" (pp. 54-55)? In the first place, making the Decalogue a series of prohibitions involves very outmoded exegesis! Furthermore, the first two commandments clearly relate to the order of purity.

In short, Belo's idea appears intriguing but too systematized, and therefore forced, inflexible, and oversimplified as he runs roughshod over the biblical texts. We will continue to encounter this problem: Belo, so scrupulous in his examination of Mark's Gospel, has an unbelievably cavalier attitude when dealing with other biblical texts. Often he knows nothing about them at all!

Another of Belo's worthwhile ideas merits further development: "the *ekklesia* is not simply the community as a gathering but also designates the *practice* specific to this community, a practice that is articulated at three levels—economic, political, and ideological—in the form of charity, hope, and faith" (p. 267). If this idea were made more explicit, I would probably agree more or less with it. In another realm, Belo and I clearly agree on the importance of emphasizing the political conflict underlying the whole Bible. But many have done so, and we will return to this matter. I also like Belo's attempt to interpret on three levels (economic, political, and ideological). But he flatters himself a bit when he presents this kind of interpretation as his creation, since it is commonplace.[4] He might retort that this pat-

---

4. Without claiming originality for my work, I could refer Belo, for example, to the introduction to my *Histoire des Institutions* (Paris: Presses

tern had never been applied to the interpretation of the Gospel. I admit it had not been done systematically and in a thorough commentary, but many works use this sort of interpretation occasionally or apply it to parts of the Bible. Finally, I also find significant and sound Belo's strict, radical opposition between God and Money, God and the State, God and Caesar, the God of the living and the God of the dead. I believe this opposition to be truly evangelical, but it is hardly original!

At this point let me make an important preliminary observation: Belo repeats widespread ideas often, believing that he is breaking new ground. About 95% of what he writes has been widely held for some time. Some examples: his theory of religion (pp. 16-19) dates from the early nineteenth century. He need not cite R. de Vaux to state that the Year of Jubilee was (probably) not observed, since this idea has been commonplace for a hundred years (carefully handed down from scholar to scholar without any proof). The heaven-earth antithesis as a basis for interpreting the two symbolic orders has also been rather widespread, since Feuerbach.[5] Another commonplace: the conflict between the prophets and Israel's political-economic system. Israel always had an earthly perspective, concerning the blessing of nature, Israel's collective destiny, etc. Belo need give us no "materialist reading" to point this fact out. The most authentically spiritual commentators of the Old Testament have often emphasized this perspective! Likewise, the idea of the temple as a political and somewhat economic center offers nothing new.

In Belo's commentary proper on Mark, we find the same sort of collection of commonplaces: Jesus as surrounded by the poor, so as to suggest the subversion of the established powers, has

---

Universitaires de France, 1955), where I analyze in detail the correlations among economics, politics, and ideology.

5. But Belo tries to base the idea of Yahweh's gift of grace on the material fact that the land is fruitful only if it receives the rain as something *given* by heaven. To establish this parallel with proper scientific rigor, he would need to *prove* that one thing always leads to the other, whereas actual experience suggests countless other interpretations. Totally divergent religious and magical systems have resulted from this observation of nature.

been a common interpretation since Tertullian. Commentators have repeatedly observed that eschatology and apocalyptic develop in an atmosphere of political powerlessness. Most of the time Belo offers us merely an elaborate repetition of the tritest interpretation (an example: Job as the book of the "problem" of individual misfortune, which remains unanswered!). Often these insights are seriously in error.[6]

I could multiply examples indefinitely. Certainly I do not blame an author for repeating earlier writers' ideas: we all resort to this practice. But I find two of Belo's tendencies unacceptable: (1) He dignifies these commonplaces with new names, using a pseudoscientific jargon that gives them the appearance of new ideas. But this newness resides only in vocabulary and labels. (2) He proclaims repeatedly: "No one has ever said this before." Perhaps not in so many words, but while he ridicules, for example, bourgeois exegesis as having misunderstood everything, he then repeats its conclusions, adding nothing fresh of his own.

2. Method

Having dispensed with these general observations, we can now begin an in-depth criticism. After a preliminary series of criticisms dealing with Belo's method, we will proceed to the essential problems.

First, Belo is incredibly sensitive to the current fashion. He uses countless acronyms to give his text a scientific flavor. For example, he writes STR Z for "strategy of the Zealots," or AA for "adversaries." This device enables him to produce wonderful combinations: "In the FS characterized by the MPE, the STR Z cannot respond to the STR AA," etc. This kind of writing

---

6. A fine example: Belo tells us that the eschatological reading of all narratives, including Israel's, reflects the formation of all narrative, the primordial narrative: "In the beginning God created. . . ." The *telos* (the end or goal) reflects the *arche* ("in the beginning"). Unfortunately, in Israel's case it does not work this way. Only a hasty, superficial reading could lead to this erroneous application. Israel does not see the end as a repetition or reproduction of the beginning! On the contrary. See my *The Meaning of the City*, trans. Dennis Pardee (Grand Rapids: Eerdmans, 1970).

is merely ridiculous and without importance: here Belo reflects R. Barthes's influence, which we can understand.

Belo has also been influenced by the popularity of plays on words, so that he gravely poses "the Problematic of K/X," which means "from Mark to Marx." I am often tempted to elaborate on such wordplay; for example, why not "from Mark to Groucho, by way of Marx: Marx (Karl) = Marx (Groucho)"? My contribution is just as valuable as his.

Belo believes in words. He thinks he has revolutionized an issue by attaching new labels to it, as I have already mentioned. Unfortunately, his "materialism" can often be reduced to use of Marxist vocabulary without genuine content, and to superimposing these words on an utterly trite presentation involving class struggle, modes of production, etc. We will return to this problem.

In addition, of course, Belo makes use of all the words currently in vogue: "strategy," "code," "system," etc. At times he becomes ridiculous, speaking gravely of "the practice of the hands or charity," "the practice of the feet or hope," and "the practice of the eyes or faith." Why speak of hands and feet, and why insist continually on Jesus' body (rejecting the idea of the person)? Only in order to despiritualize or materialize. This way, when he speaks of the body and its activity and practice, he can consider himself a materialist![7] But Marx called this approach "phraseological materialism" (in *The German Ideology*). Belo arrives at this "materialism" only by neglecting important matters; for instance, he appears unaware of the radical antithesis (dating from the seventh century B.C.) between sight and faith. The eyes *cannot* function as the organ of faith or its expression, etc. Belo's neglect of this absolute contradiction shows that he is basically ignorant of the specificity of Israel's "religion."

When Belo refers to Jesus' comment on the poor widow's mite, he again descends to the ridiculous. He declares gravely

---

7. I might point out to Belo that this sort of materialism amounts to exactly the opposite of Marx's understanding of materialism. Belo rejoins B. F. Skinner's behaviorist concept at this point—Skinner, the fine American bourgeois pro-capitalist who does not let this "materialist practice of the body" bother him in the slightest!

that at this point we remain in "the economic register" (p. 193), and that Jesus has "given a lesson in subversion of economic practice in the area of ecclesiality"! Obviously, Belo does not know what Marx means by "economic practice"!

To continue with Belo's vocabulary, I find two of his tendencies disturbing: (1) He arbitrarily ascribes whatever meaning he pleases to words, only to believe afterward that he has demonstrated something. (2) At the same time, he uses modern words with a strong emotional connotation in order to ascribe overtones indirectly to the text.

Concerning the first of these two tendencies, he gives a whole series of definitions in Part I (for forces of production, practice, relations of production, mode of production, mode of circulation, etc.), using well-defined Marxist vocabulary, to which he *gives different meanings*. It would take a Marxist's breath away. I consider this practice irresponsible and dishonest. Concerning Belo's second tendency, the arbitrary use of emotionally charged words, he translates the Greek *pais* as "youths" rather than as "children," which would not fit in with his intentions! The "youth" must represent a force.

In another case, Belo insists that the Greek verb for Jesus' death means "murder," whereas it means "kill." The idea that Jesus did not *die* but was the victim of a *murder* matters to Belo (see p. 227 and notes). Reducing the event to a death reflects bourgeois ideology, which tries to spiritualize and cover over the conflict. So we must speak of "murder." Unfortunately, the word "murder" has a precise meaning that fails to fit the (unjust) condemnation by a "legitimate" government. Shifting from one word to the other constitutes in itself an ideological process, parallel to the bourgeois interpretation's process. Other examples of loaded words: Belo refers to "a protest meeting" held by Jesus (p. 192), and to "guerrillas" rather than rebels or robbers. Elsewhere he finds that "neighbor" in Jesus' teaching *always* means a poor person (after the rich young man leaves).

Furthermore, he speaks pompously (but in this Belo has lots of company!) of "textual production" rather than of composition or writing. This switch in terminology is clearly no accident: it means to affirm indirectly that the text is a "product" comparable to any industrial product, so that we can analyze it in terms of the Marxist approach to the modes of production. We can affirm that a literary text relates to a historical context and a social group, reflects a given ideology, etc. But Belo ignores the enormous distance between these facts and the affirmation that a text is subject to the laws of industrial production. These laws involve division of labor (internal rather than overall division of labor—this difference has escaped Belo); means of technical production; constant, circulating, and fixed capital; etc. Belo's clever effort to confuse the reader keeps him from mentioning these matters, but he treats the text as if it were subject to these factors. We have here, then, a continual use of loaded words, intended to make the reader swallow a whole series of images, without realizing it.

Belo's entire argument depends on a certain number of ideological *presuppositions* he holds firmly but never demonstrates. Faith is an ideology, he believes. Everything related to "heaven," the "Spirit," etc., he calls "mythology." Only materialism is scientific, and the only science of history is historical materialism. Work is the key to all reality, since production explains everything, etc. We have here an implicit creed, founded on Belo's adherence by faith to a given interpretation, which I would not dare describe as Marxist. Belo takes for scientific truths those things he finds evident, but which I would feel obliged to call mythical, since they are neither based on reason nor critically examined.

This defect comes clearly to light when we consider Belo on the idea of classes and class struggle. He believes classes have always existed, in all societies and circumstances. They are a "given"; he makes no effort to prove they exist. Any time you have two different groups, one of which dominates the other, they are "classes." We will come back to this problem.

We still have two methodological questions to consider. The first is the problem of Belo's "frames of reference" (to use the pretentious terminology in vogue!). His book presents us with an astonishing mixture of conflicting inspirations. Belo refers and admits to four major sources: L. Althusser, structuralism, G. Bataille, and F. Nietzsche. Certainly, in an essay or meditation, the author may refer to a source and borrow ideas from various writers. But since Belo claims to do a rigorous, strictly scientific study, he should not borrow ideas in this work.

On the one hand, he makes partial use of the structuralist method, and on the other hand, he gives a Marxist materialist reading, since the concepts he uses and formulates are Marx's. But Belo appears not to suspect their incompatibilities: Marx's thought is a whole—a precise, integrated unit, based on a thorough method. Once one has adopted it, one cannot mix it with other methods and concepts. Belo has no idea of the basic contradiction between structuralism and Marx's method and thought. Lefebvre has clearly demonstrated this insoluble contradiction.[8]

The place of history furnishes us with an especially good example: not by accident does Belo adopt the division (unthinkable for Marx) between historical materialism and dialectical materialism. Not by accident does he redefine Marx's concepts and appropriate them. Doesn't Belo see that in so doing he destroys Marx's methodology? And if he claims to establish one of his own in its place, he must rigorously demonstrate and establish it. But this he fails to do, trusting in his presupposition that the Marxist (materialist) method is rigorous, but also that the structuralist-linguistic method is rigorous. By not seeing their contradiction, he arrives at monstrous conclusions, some of which we will examine.

Likewise, Belo introduces some of Nietzsche's concepts. I do not maintain that Nietzsche is systematic, but how can anyone combine his thought with that of Marx?[9] What can be the purpose of introducing ideas like the will to power or the eternal return into Marx's interpretation of history? Belo concocts a patchwork of the notions that have attracted him, offering us a

---

8. H. Lefebvre, *Le Nouvel Eléatisme* (1971).

9. To be sure, Belo has perceived the outrageousness of combining Nietzsche and Marx (pp. 271-72), but his five footnotes resolve nothing. In particular, his unwarranted change of "labor power" to "forces" and then to "relation of forces" enables him, incredibly, to identify the Marxist concept of labor force with Nietzsche's "will to power." Also incredible: his similar attempt to reduce Nietzsche's subjectivity to a set of tactics that takes the collusion of agents into account.

hodgepodge of ideas (with something for everyone) as if they were a coordinated whole.

Finally, I would like to make two observations about the laxity of Belo's "method." (1) He confuses the reader continually (he is not alone in this). For example, he considers an institution in Israel and proceeds to confuse it with institutions of the same *name* in other cultures. He fails to take Israel's peculiarities into account (in other words, he fails to take history into account!). He equates Jewish royalty with the other royalties of the Near East. Slavery he sees as the same everywhere.

Belo reduces the entire law to the system of pollution and debt ("pollution" in the sense used, of course, in the generalizations of socioanthropological studies). Belo never asks himself if pollution in Israel differs from what is called "pollution" elsewhere. In other words, he equates things that cannot always be equated, erasing their differences and hastily identifying them.

We find this same laxity and confusion when Belo speaks of "Communism" and the Communist revolution. He can of course declare that Jesus' messianic practice is a radically Communist strategy (he can say anything he likes!), but he should at least indicate that this "Communism" has nothing to do with Marx's, since it in no way results from an evolution of the forces of production. Based on this confusion, Belo arrives at conclusions quite acceptable on an emotional level, but completely impossible to affirm from a Marxist perspective.[10]

This way of confusing the reader is not new: it follows an overall interpretation, decided on in advance. It uses texts and words simply to bolster an argument. Belo's version of this approach manipulates the Gospel of Mark and Jesus so as to authorize and prop up the author's personal ideology.

(2) My final preliminary remark concerns Belo's method-

---

10. For instance, Belo says that one aspect of present-day Communist strategy would consist of reformulating the proletarian utopia, which had money as its fetish. Products as a "body" would replace the economic utopia. But this is utterly unacceptable as an interpretation of Marx. No such reformulation of a (nonexistent!) utopia is possible, and this particular change could take place only as a result of the maturing of the prior economic system.

ological casualness. Usually he follows Marx. When Marx
seems cumbersome, however, or his conclusions do not fit, Belo
abandons him without hesitation, and without considering the
lack of consistency involved.

Even stranger is Belo's attitude toward bourgeois exegesis.
Usually he finds it erroneous, because it is ideological. Many
times Belo remarks that bourgeois historians and exegetes have
understood nothing about the Gospel or Jesus' practice. But
from time to time, without explanation, Belo incorporates these
exegetes' conclusions, as if they were automatically acceptable.
For instance, Belo believes the "genuine" text of Mark ends at
16:8, so that verses 9-20 are excluded. His argument: "Everyone
is agreed that Mark 16:9-20 . . . does not belong to the text"
(p. 233). Everyone? These unacceptable bourgeois exegetes are
precisely those who agree on ending the text at verse 8. Here,
suddenly, their authority becomes obvious. Why? Only because
it suits Belo's argument for the text of Mark to end at this particular point.

Belo often has recourse to using bourgeois theological arguments because he needs them. Another strange example: on the
whole, Belo considers Matthew's Gospel as theologically reworked and therefore "conformist." But when he needs to prove
that Jesus Himself was a "violent" figure who knew "class
struggle" well, Belo recommends reading Matthew 23 "aloud as
if you were an actor, and you will end up red-faced and full of
violent feeling. Matthew is showing us a real protest meeting.
Let no one try to tell us that Jesus was meek and nonviolent or
that he was ignorant of the class struggle" (p. 326, n. 146). In
other words, since this text squares with the picture Belo wants
to give, he takes it to be authentic.

What has happened to the author's contention that we must
not concern ourselves with the words themselves? What a
strange way to do things: we either have a theological text reworked to tally with bourgeois ideology, in which case it fails to
reflect Jesus' words, or else we have Jesus' words. But how
could we recognize them unless we had a model for what Jesus
was like? How could His words have been inadvertently preserved within a text completely reworked to make Jesus say the
opposite of what He really said? How does Belo know these are

really Jesus' words? His implicit reasoning: theological discourse is conformist (that is, it agrees with the ruling class); this text is not conformist; since Jesus was a revolutionary, this text gives us His genuine words.

On this basis, we see how another circular argument develops: the premise resulting from the reasoning I have just outlined is that this text is something Jesus actually said, since it is a revolutionary declaration. Here is the secondary argument: read this text to see how revolutionary Jesus was! The fallacy of Belo's "method" is clear. In the Gospels as well as in the other sources he uses, Belo selects what serves his argument and rejects what contradicts it, however he likes.

3. Materialism

We now approach the central issues of our debate. Belo claims to give us a materialist reading of the Gospel. I confess I have searched for the materialist element in this book without finding it. What do we mean by materialism? Many definitions can be offered:

(1) The decision to deny the Spirit, the Transcendent, life after death, and especially a "God" intervening in history. This monistic philosophical decision can also be methodological: any historian interpreting a text would certainly place God's intervention within parentheses. Scientifically, one cannot relate a given action or event to God. Such a practice betrays no necessarily materialist prejudice: any bourgeois historian, even a spiritualist, would use the same method.

(2) Every historical process has an economic basis. In this case as well, for a century or more, there has been no need to be a materialist to agree! Explaining history on the basis of economics has become a commonplace.

(3) A society is primarily characterized by class relationships and class struggle. Here again, in spite of what some say, we have an idea that is not necessarily materialist. Before Marx affirmed this, A. Turgot (1727-81) used the idea and these terms to explain societal change; his theory was completed by L. Thiers (in his *Histoire du Consulat et de l'Empire,* 1840).

(4) Much more recently, scholars have claimed to follow

materialism when they research the conditions of the "production" of a text (its class, relations of force, etc.). But again in this
case they wrap a very old approach in modern dress: Taine gave
the best explanation of this method. And the fact that utterly
bourgeois historians, with little Leftist commitment, practice
this approach shows it is not truly materialist.

Belo confuses classical historical study with the materialist
historical method. In his work, he has no need to declare himself a materialist, since he uses no specifically materialist historical method.[11] With respect to the four points enumerated above,
genuine materialism would consist of a *closed* and *absolute* pos-
ture. That is, one would affirm that no other factor can inter-
vene. According to this stance, history is constituted by the
forces in question (history rather than the science of history),
and nothing else can enter in. The "God" factor is excluded not
only by interpretation, but also by any factual possibility.
Another example of the absolute position: the economic factor
explains *everything* that takes place, excluding any independent
spirituality. And another: the material conditions of the production of the text exclude any other factor in its creation. In other
words, *materialism exists only where there is exclusivity.*

Anyone can see that a metaphysical choice is involved
here—a kind of wager in Pascal's terms, but on the opposite
side. A simple affirmation takes place. The materialist option (in
this sense) is just as impossible to prove as the spiritualist option (and Marx knew this so well he never tried to prove the
materialist option). As a result, the science in question depends
on an irrational, preliminary choice.

Belo makes no other radical choices in his book. At times he
gives the impression that materialism is basic: everything is reduced to strategies, forces of production, relations of force, etc.
At other times, quite ambiguously, he maintains the intervention of the Spirit, without explaining what he means. Concerning the resurrection, his style is so slippery we cannot determine
if, on the one hand, he reduces the resurrection to the "succes-

---

11. His method for interpreting the text of Mark is much closer to
structuralism and linguistics, as exemplified by Barthes and J. Derrida.
But I will risk no criticism in this area, since I would be out of my field.

sion of disciples," or to political insurrection, or if, on the other
hand, he holds to a specific resurrection of Jesus' body.

In short, Belo apparently presents the simple well-known
historical method as "materialist" and leaves us in the dark with
respect to his belief in a rigorous and consistent materialism. His
interpretation's value lies in his rejection of the easy way out: of
the so-called spiritualist interpretation, which resolves all problems by resorting to the Holy Spirit's inspiration. But many of
us nonmaterialists agree on this point!

4. Marxism

At this point we come to the painful part of our critique. Obviously, in order to develop a materialist method of interpretation, one must determine exactly which material factors determined the elaboration of the text. The author means to use our
available knowledge of the socioeconomic milieu in the
Palestine of Jesus' time. Belo appears not to realize, however, the
incredible difficulty faced by historians who wish to uncover all
the factors and put them into play with each other. A further
complication: concentration on one moment in time cannot suffice; one must take developments into account.[12]

Thus, Belo tries to determine the factors of the Hellenistic
world in Judea at Jesus' time, or at the time of the writing of
Mark's Gospel. But between A.D. 30 and 70 profound transfor-
mations took place. Belo dispenses with them in one fell swoop:
they are merely details for the erudite! But can one claim to
study the "conditions of the production of a text" based on a few
generalities, some vague approximations, and quickly drawn
overviews? My criticism involves mainly this: if someone seeks
to show the influence of material factors and the meaning of the
text as it relates to these factors, he must know them completely
and precisely. I also contend such knowledge is impossible,

---

12. Such variations are essential. "Capitalism," for instance, is not always the same, and present variations within capitalism have provoked
contemporary dissensions within Marxism. But Belo remains untouched
by such considerations: he "scientifically" applies Marx's writings concerning nineteenth-century capitalism to first-century Roman "capitalism"!

given the present state of the science of history. But Belo seems unaware of this entire problem.

However unspecialized a historian may be, he cannot fail to react with amazement at Belo's factual errors, lacunae, naïveté, and excesses, since they occur on practically every page. I am well aware that Belo indicates he is not a historical scholar and that he must rely on secondary sources. Certainly we should not fault him for this dependence. But he relies on sources four or five times removed from the originals![13] Furthermore, Belo takes ideological generalizations for history (example: G. le Dhoquois, *Pour l'histoire*). And although correct, well-constructed secondary sources can serve as the basis for a study like Belo's, the use of such fourthhand works is dangerous.

Belo's enormous lacunae seem to me to occur mainly in two areas: Marx's thought, which Belo obviously knows only as filtered through Althusser's interpretation, and the historical and economic conditions in Judea, which he knows only by way of theoretical generalizations (with the exception of the excellent book by S. Baron). Belo's lacunae and what we must call his ignorance seem striking considering his erudition with respect to other sources: he knows J. Derrida, Althusser, G. von Rad, R. de Vaux, and others quite well. But this list of authors reveals an important fact: Belo knows *recent* books well, but appears *completely ignorant of what came before them*. As I have said, he does not know Marx, but he is saturated with Althusser. We get the unhappy impression of a thin film of present-day erudition

---

13. By way of clarification: in the field of history a source is primary when based on personal, direct reading of witnesses, papyri, ostraca, etc. Naturally these are very specialized works. Secondary sources are more general and provide an updated synthesis of knowledge in a given area, using primary sources. Thirdhand sources use secondary sources to form a wider, more generalized, overview (for example, a treatise on economic history or on an entire era, etc.). Fourthhand sources give a vast overview (examples: A. Toynbee or Jacques Pirenne). Fifthhand sources provide ideological or theoretical interpretations, attempting to give the meaning or explanation of a given historical whole (for example, Engels's work on Gibbon's history, itself a thirdhand source).

floating on a sea of ignorance. I shall give several examples; it would be impossible to give them all!

Belo attributes to Althusser the distinction between dialectical materialism and historical materialism. He seems unaware that Stalin originated this distinction and that an enormous debate on the subject took place among Marxist theoreticians between 1936 and 1946. For some, Stalin's theoretical errors stem precisely from this distinction. Marx, however, makes no such differentiation: history is dialectical, and materialism is *both* dialectical *and* historical.

Belo often gives utterly arbitrary definitions for terms used by Marxism. For example, he distorts Marx's concept when he states that the relation of production is "the relation of economic ownership between the appropriators of the surplus economic products and the means of production" (p. 9). He distinguishes this idea from juridical property, which has to do with political action. Thus Belo doubly distorts Marx's concept, since production relations constitute the entire economic structure of society (and thus all social relationships *in the area of work*), and his term "surplus economic products" has no meaning. Production of *added* value exists, but we cannot speak of "surplus." These apparently slight distortions can hardly be considered accidental, however, since such vague but inaccurate usage enables Belo to speak of a "subasiatic mode of production," as we will see.

Similarly, Belo offers an astonishing definition for practice, taken over from Althusser, but after eliminating its economic aspect. Marx's "praxis" is identical with this "practice"; but the fact that Marx held to the term "praxis" shows that he meant something quite different from mere practice. Belo reduces Marx's "praxis," a difficult and rigorous concept, to "any process of *transformation* of a determinate given raw material into a determinate *product,* a transformation effected by a determinate human labour, using determinate means" (p. 7). Thus Belo enlarges Marx's concept beyond the economic sphere and the production of *value.*

On the contrary, in Marx, praxis, related to theory, is the means of transforming the world and of making history, through work of a technical and economic sort. Once Belo has redefined "practice" so vaguely, he can speak blithely about "political practice" or "ideological practice." These terms mean something in ordinary and journalistic language, but not within the rigorous sphere of Marx's thought. We can say the same for Belo's "messianic practice" and "subversive practice."

Belo's abandonment of the exclusively economic tenor of the term "praxis" shows how little he values materialism. Marx would have roared furiously at Belo's transposition in which "messianic practice" is "a process of *transforming* a given raw material (economic, political, and ideological relations . . .) into a product (new . . . relations . . .), a transformation effected by human labor (the practice of the body of J[esus]), using certain means of production" (p. 253). Considering how Marx treated B. Bauer, we can imagine the ridicule he would have heaped on Belo's indefensible concoction, which amounts to a mere combination of words with no precise meaning. In this messianic context we cannot speak of production or of means of production, except, as we have said, in ordinary language or journalistic commonplaces. But in this case the concept cannot serve as the kind of intellectual structure Belo proposes.

This leads us to our most serious criticism in this area. Belo repeats Dhoquois's "classification" of differing modes of production: Asiatic, subasiatic, paraasiatic, Asiatic feudalist, etc. (pp. 26-27). Belo classifies the Jewish economy as subasiatic. Here I feel I must react strongly. We all know Marx and Engels's rather rigorous progression, going from the primitive commune to the mode of production based on slavery, then to the feudal mode of production, and finally to the capitalist mode. M. Godelier, in particular, has emphasized two texts in which Marx and Engels underline another possible model, which they call the Asiatic mode of production. This model would have the possibility of a different evolution; it could, in particular, jump one or another of the above stages to arrive at capitalism. The Asiatic mode of production is characterized by the production of consumer goods (at the practical level) for families, villages, and communities. Since the entire economy depends on collective organization (large projects such as irrigation), involving government mobilization of all available manpower and appropriation of land, this model involves political power over the totality of the means of production.

The Asiatic mode of production, however, involves the intervention of a strong central power that deducts part of people's income through these projects, *which alone make possible* the activities of production at the village level. As always in Marx, the system has its explanation and its legitimation: this is not simply "state" violence. Speaking of a subasiatic model, therefore, is meaningless where no collective projects exist in the economic infrastructure. Yet Belo uses the term to designate a society in which the political power intervenes by deducting part of the "surplus products" (but without any legitimation and by purely violent means) and by controlling the economy (but do we assume this concept presupposes the production of merchandise?).

All this has no meaning in terms of Marx's thought, in which the "mode of production" involves specificity of *both* the forces of technical production *and* production relations (thus one can legitimately speak of an Asiatic mode of production). But in Belo's book only production relations are involved. Furthermore, it is ridiculous to speak of "surplus products" when the forces of production are not transformed into merchandise.

For the sake of specialists, I could enter into more detail in these criticisms. We have here, in brief, the use of words with no content. Yet such words give the appearance of erudition and of a connection with Marx's thought. Obviously, Belo could respond: "I make no pretense of fidelity to Marx's thought." But in this case, why does he use all the Marxist vocabulary, and apparently Marxist reasoning; why does he claim to give a Marxist type of theoretical foundation? If he does not intend to be faithful to Marx's thought, why does he talk about "scientific materialism"?

In such a context, rigorous logic is called for, yet Belo merely exercises his imagination. In reality, he deals with societies whose production is exclusively of the rural, village, communal, or family type. Superimposed on this structure we have various kinds of political power, which deduct economic wealth in exchange for certain services (collective protection, for example; it is absurd to call this relation mere oppression and violence!). But this structure does not constitute a model of mode of production, since the political power is in no way integrated into the circuit of production.

When we recall Marx's meticulous analyses designed to de-

termine all aspects, characteristics, and specificities of a mode
of production (feudal, for example), and also his effort to show
that a mode of production presupposes the integration of all factors into a whole, and that multiple relationships exist among
the factors, we are simply stupefied by Belo's frivolousness. His
labels, such as "subasiatic" and "Asiatic feudalism," are totally
lacking in consistency. One cannot possibly say that Israel's concept of property was "Asiatic," since no collective project was
organized along centralized lines with a view to production.

5. Social Classes and the State

These issues lead us to consider two particularly flagrant errors.
Belo speaks continually of "classes" and the "state" when he is
talking about Israel. Serious objections have been made on both
these points, although I admit Belo is following a common practice in his usage here. Can we speak of a "state" whenever we
are considering a political power? In reality, this practice is in-
defensibly casual. How can we possibly compare the charismatic power of a Romulus with the enormous bureaucratic organization of a modern state? Or the Merovingian patrimonial
system with the Athenian aristocracy's legal system? These errors amount to the same thing as calling all mammals "human."

We must limit the word "state" to the abstract, juridical,
bureaucratic, and anonymous organization of the modern state,
using the wider expression "political power" for the totality of
the forms of power (including the state). But this practice would
destroy several of Belo's arguments, since he plays continually
on the ambiguity of the word "state" in order to slip very modern characteristics into his explanation of the organization of
Jewish political power. As a result, he completely eliminates any
historical dimension, abolishes all specificity of political forms,
and makes arbitrary generalizations (his explanation of absolute monarchy on p. 13, for instance, is unhistorical and quite
amusing!).

We run into the same problem when Belo supposes the existence of social classes in all societies (although he tries to define
everything, he does not bother to define social classes—surely
everyone knows what they are!). But when we consider his text

in detail, we are in for a surprise. First, it seems obvious to him that the distinction between rich and poor, or between the politically dominant and the dominated, corresponds to a class division. He appears unaware of the many texts in which Marx inveighs against just such confusion. Social classes in Marx definitely do not correspond to a class of poor people and a class of rich people, or of those who hold political power, etc. Furthermore, Marx gives abundant reasons to show why this is so!

Belo's reasoning is also hazy as he continually substitutes *caste* for *class*. He appears unaware that these are two utterly contradictory realities. "Class" in Marx involves a precise analysis of the structures of the forces of production in opposition to the relations of production and cannot refer to any social stratum whatever or to groups in general, even if they are in conflict. Nor can it refer to the presence of invaders (Marx explains, for example, why the Franks in seventh-century France are merely invaders rather than a social class!). A "class" is not produced in every economic and social context.

Belo appears unaware of these matters, however. For him, "class" means a kind of metaphysical entity which needs no definition and whose existence is obvious. Therefore Israel has classes. Here again we find something amusing. According to Belo, Israel's priests and King David's military officers are classes! What is their role in economic production? None at all. But no matter! How is such a class constituted? "The king actually did conscript the young men of the country population in order to put them in his garrisons as regular soldiers. He laid hands on landed property to set up estates of his own throughout the country; and from the country population, too, he drew the labour forces for these estates. Other landed property he confiscated as rewards for his henchmen" (pp. 55-56, quoting von Rad). Thus is a ruling class constituted! Belo believes David founds a class system in this way. Incredible! When we know how fragile and parasitical this military-political stratum was, we cannot possibly speak of "class struggle," since as a social category this group has no control over the forces of production. It neither owns all Israel's land nor does it organize production. Belo's approach is pseudo-Marxist and pseudo-materialist.

6. History

Now we move to the second large area of Belo's lacunae and errors. In general we should fault his incredibly superficial knowledge of the juridical and political organization in Judea in Jesus' time, as well as of the economic situation.

In the latter area, Belo falls continually into the trap of using a label ("subasiatic move of production") to replace precise knowledge of the facts. Clearly he is utterly unacquainted with studies of the economy of the period (F. Heichelheim, Tenney Frank, M. Rostovtzeff, J. Valarché, to mention only the classics, each of whom provided us with a precise vision of Middle Eastern or Roman economy for the period in question). Most of all, he fails to note the monumental *Cambridge Economic History*. How can Belo possibly claim to speak of forces of production, production relations, economic structure, etc., without at least knowing the facts? By this I do not mean that Belo should have impressed us uselessly with his erudition. I merely bring up an essential problem: one can make generalizations and attempt to explain things only by building on a foundation of the most precise knowledge possible, exactly as Marx did!

I could point out many errors in this connection, but I will mention only two, as examples. Like many others, Belo classifies the "publicans" with the poor. He believes Jesus drew into His entourage only the poor and those who resisted the Romans. But this view betrays astounding ignorance. We have no reason to believe that the biblical text has departed from the normal meaning for "publican" in the case of Levi, Zacchaeus, etc., since the term used, *telones,* is the specific word for a tax collector rather than for an employee. Publicans were rich people— *the* financial power of the empire.

Everything depended on the tax collection system. Since Rome had no civil service (Augustus inaugurated it, and here again, when Belo happens to mention the Roman governors, he furnishes us with a portrait that was correct until 14 B.C., but which no longer held true forty years later), taxes were farmed out. Thus an individual paid in advance to the Roman treasury an estimate of what given taxes should bring, and then collected the taxes on his own account. His profit was the difference between what he had paid the treasury at the beginning of the year and what he had collected by year's end. Beginning in the second century B.C., the publicans contracted for large amounts of taxes; in order to pay the large amounts required by the treasury, tax collectors joined forces to form enormous financial companies. Augustus attempted to break this capitalist power and to divide tax collection into smaller fragments.

Thus a person with enough wealth could contract for the customs collection at a given place in the empire or for the toll at the entrance and exit of cities. Colossal sums were clearly not required, but certainly an individual had to possess a large fortune to be able to pay in advance the equivalent of the toll (4%) on all merchandise for a year. This was the situation of our famous publicans.

Their distress consisted of being detested by everyone (since they had to be demanding in order to make a profit) and of being collaborators of the invader. Belo, who is so fond of modern equivalents, should have pointed out, for example, that the publicans were the equivalent of those who collaborated with the Germans in 1940-44, who became rich through their transactions with the invaders and through exploitation of the poor. But in this case, of course, the classic picture Belo draws of class struggle would not have held true!

In contrast, Jesus' following strikes us by its heterogeneity: it included poor *and rich*, nationalistic Zealots *and* collaborators. But with his ideological bias, Belo could not see this diversity.

We cannot stop to consider at length all the issues of this sort raised in Belo's book. We should remind ourselves, however, that the prostitutes mentioned in the Gospels cannot be compared with poor streetwalkers loitering in ports of call and subject to pimps (we know a great deal about the status of prostitutes under the Seleucids). The prostitutes of the Gospels correspond instead to modern "call girls," and were rich (although obviously despised).

Speaking of peasants, Belo uses an outrageous phrase: "they each had equal value as agents of production, and this fact made the feudal political relationship evident: they were easily swapped or bartered." Here Belo betrays his amazing ignorance. Under a feudal system one of the most general characteristics of peasants is just the opposite: attached to the land, they cannot be moved or uprooted by their lord (except under very exceptional circumstances)! Furthermore, we can legitimately ask how Belo could locate a "feudal" regime at the time and place he writes about!

Naturally, Belo subscribes to the commonly held notion that the Roman empire maintained its power only through its very strong army. He is unaware, of course, of the extent to which Rome kept its army small. No, the empire did not depend on the army, but on its administrative ability and on the consent of the overwhelming majority of the empire's peoples (here Belo will accuse me of being a Rightist bourgeois ideologist).

Belo should know that for the Romans Judea represented an incomprehensible abcess in the midst of a generally calm empire, since otherwise local populations felt satisfied. Not without reason did this one province change its political and administrative status three times in seventy-five years: the Romans tried out every method, attempting to reduce with a minimum of violence an opposition they failed to understand, since they did not encounter it elsewhere. Their usual tactic, when they met with basic and enduring opposition stemming from the people, involved backing off and leaving the nation involved outside the empire: for example, the Picts, Batavians, and Dacians.

Judea was a different matter, however: the Romans had thrust their conquest as far as the boundary of the Parthian empire. They could not leave Judea out—and it was the only place they met with violent popular opposition. If there had been ten Judeas in the empire, it would have folded within ten years! We must realize that in order to conduct the war of A.D. 67-70, the Romans had to assemble half their entire army, thus leaving most of their provinces and boundaries defenseless! This was necessary because the Roman part of the army amounted to only about twenty-five legions (not counting the auxiliaries).

Belo's minor errors accumulate endlessly. On page 225, for example, he suggests that dressing Jesus in purple amounted to dressing him like a soldier! Astonishingly, Belo fails to note that the purple cloak was reserved for the general in chief and the emperor; in this passage (Mark 15:17) we must be dealing with the red cloak of a centurion; if a soldier wore it, he was severely punished. The cross becomes for Belo the torture of guerrillas, whereas it was the way of executing *slaves*, used only exceptionally for cases of rebellion to dramatize the slave status of the prisoner.

Belo appears unaware of the importance of the term *savior* (Greek *soter*) in the Middle East. This seems odd, since it would have provided him with additional ammunition. When Jesus is called *soter*, a political proclamation by the opposition is involved; since the third century B.C., the Seleucid kings had used the title of Benefactor *(euergete)* and Savior. In spite of his refusal, the title was attributed to Augustus, and later unofficially to other emperors, as successors of the Seleucids. In other words, this title amounts to political opposition rather than religious terminology.

I will mention only a few examples of Belo's ignorance of history, but in general history fails to interest him: he downgrades it quite simply, for example, by saying twice that the conflict over slavery is so severe that it causes the rapid collapse of the empire, "although it manages to resist for a time"! Amazing: it will take five hundred years to destroy the empire, but in Belo's view, this is a short time! This period involves brilliant centuries, nonetheless, that dazzle from every point of view, including economically, such as the century of the Antonines. We might as well say "Yes, capitalism appears in the sixteenth century, but its internal contradictions are such that it soon collapses, although it manages to resist for a time." Between 1500 and our day, after all, much has taken place!

Similarly, Belo generalizes from a statement by G. Alfaric, contending that all notion of a mother country disappeared in the empire, leaving only an awful mixture of widely divergent traditions, an assortment of clans and tribes assembled by the Romans. But the issue here is *when* this became true: Belo's assertion could apply to the fourth century, but it is totally false for Jesus' time, the era to which Belo applies it.

Such historical ignorance leads Belo to make naïve or simplistic statements, particularly when he tries to be original and to attack bourgeois historians who "cannot understand." Some examples: he uses a classical interpretation of the expression "Son of God," but insists that bourgeois exegetes cannot comprehend it because they begin with a ready-made reading grid instead of the analytical code. He establishes the obvious relationship between Jesus' prayer and action, claiming no one has been able to explain it, since bourgeois ideologues think they already know what prayer is, but are mistaken.

Concerning the feeding of the five thousand, Belo again provides us with an extremely well-known interpretation, found in a hundred sermons. But not according to him: his reading amounts to a remarkable innovation, since bourgeois exegesis has presented this miracle as a sign of the coming Kingdom, or else an allusion to the Eucharist. Of course, some exegetes have made these points, but we have also seen Belo's approach used!

He takes the old chestnut dating from Ernest Renan and Alfred Loisy, that the difference between what the evangelists (especially Luke) said about the Parousia and what Jesus may have said (and more generally the theological changes that occurred between A.D. 50 and 100) reflects the Parousia's delay. Belo attributes this "discovery" to H. Conzelmann, but it can be found in all the biblical introductions—a typical example of Belo's erudition, based on recent books, and involving fundamental ignorance.

Belo presents as something new the insight that the conflict building up around Jesus was political in nature. Jesus opposed the rich, the Romans, the powerful, and the temple (as an economic center). According to Belo, bourgeois exegesis never managed to uncover this insight, having rarely asked questions about the political reasons for Jesus' death! The reader thinks he is dreaming at this point, since Belo offers us the most common interpretation by far. I could refer him, for example, to studies of Jesus' trial by historians of institutions (see J. Imbert's bibliography), who have never doubted the political nature of the event.

A final example (but we could go on endlessly): in connection with Jesus' arrest, Belo speaks correctly of His temptation to defend Himself by force. This point seems rather obvious, considering the incident involving the sword, Jesus' prayer in Gethsemane, and his "Do you think that I cannot appeal to my Father, and he will at once send me more than twelve legions of

angels?" (Matt. 26:53). But Belo declares that "Bourgeois exegetes . . . are unable to read that J[esus] could have been
tempted at this level" (p. 328, n. 178). In reality, Belo considers
exegetes imbeciles rather than bourgeois! How many theologians have written over the last two thousand years that Jesus,
during His arrest and on the cross, met with a temptation similar to the one in the desert?

In summary, Belo's ignorance concerning scientific matters
does not bother me much, since we all share that problem. Two
other matters trouble me much more: (1) his view that others
interpret ideologically, and can therefore not understand the
text. Since he is the first to provide a scientific interpretation, he
offers something no one has said before; and (2) the necessity
of beginning with a knowledge of historical facts if one is to establish the conditions of a text's "production." This analysis
cannot be accomplished on the basis of a previously chosen interpretation that bears no relationship with reality. The "materialist reading" of the text stemming from such an interpretation serves only as apparent confirmation—just as we might
have expected!

The criticisms in the areas of historical, economic, and Marxist knowledge I have outlined here are not intended as a display
of erudition. I do not take the stance of a literary critic who
would reproach an author for failing to know something. Nor
is my criticism meant to be limited to this particular book by
Belo. I have tried to show the fundamental impossibility of carrying out his project of a completely materialist reading of the
Bible and a materialist theology. I say "fundamental impossibility" because the project is contradictory in itself, since it involves an overall interpretation based on a true knowledge of
the facts. The idealist interpretation was not "good," but it involved a coherent project: an overall construction based on, and
as a function of, ideas, and this kind of project remains possible.

In Belo's case, however, we are dealing with the reality of
historical fact, at least if we limit ourselves to historical materialism (and all other materialism amounts to idealism!). But even
the best and most exacting specialists realize that they know
only a small portion of these historical facts. For this reason,
they hesitate to risk publishing syntheses, and in any case leave

such attempts open to revision. Certainly, the state of our knowledge does not allow us to undertake a vast overall explanation based on historical facts. For this reason, it is so much more tempting to substitute formulas, oversimplifications, and ready-made ideas for historical reality. No other building blocks are available to the person who tries to construct a materialist explanation of the Gospels or a materialist theology. Belo's work unintentionally bears this fact out!

7. Implications

Using two examples, I want to introduce a final order of criticism: at times Belo seems not to realize fully the implications of his proposals. For instance, he complains rightly about the spiritualization of the Gospels (but this is no longer really such a problem). Then he tells us that the crowd's eating to satisfaction in the feeding of the five thousand should be understood in a material sense (Mark 6:42; here Belo rightly insists, p. 140, that the narrative emphasizes the "filling" rather than a "multiplication"). Agreed. But he extends the idea: Jesus is recognized as Messiah because He has (materially) satisfied the crowds. This narrative shows, according to Belo, the nonspirituality of Jesus the Messiah: His political, economic, and ideological character. The action of giving bread to the poor becomes the essential element—*the* messianic act. This (economic) practice ("Give whatever you have to the poor") becomes Jesus' very body, which will remain present only through this practice, which is concrete and not symbolic.

Belo then protests when a commentator claims that although material hunger is doubtless important, it is not the only hunger. For Belo, it is the only hunger. And the messianic movement based on the satisfaction of hunger proclaims "the collective Son of man." Thus we are oriented toward "a political strategy aimed at the worldwide table at which the poor are filled" (this is the hope). I am sorry to point out that this perspective has already been thoroughly described by F. Dostoyevski, in "The Grand Inquisitor" *(The Brothers Karamazov)*. If the only problem is the (material) satisfaction of the crowds, and a worldwide strategy the only substitute, then the only one who will effectively accomplish it is the Grand Inquisitor. Belo fails utterly to realize the historical consequences of what he writes, and the connection between this project and the second temptation!

Another example of such oversight: Belo speaks continually, in fashionable language, of "strategy." He shows the strategy of the crowd, of the Zealots, of Jesus, of the adversaries, of the Romans, etc. Faith is defined as a little strategy for approaching Jesus.[14] Belo rightly shows the difference between Jesus' strategy and that of the Zealots. But the reader puzzles somewhat over Belo's understanding of Jesus' strategy: it "was the radical subversion of the code of the SOC [social code]" (p. 261). Whether we like it or not, a strategy is not just a way of doing things or a series of positions adopted: "strategy" implies organizing action with a view to victory. This is especially true when we speak (as Belo does in Jesus' case) of political strategy. Belo confirms this point by saying that a clandestine strategy presupposes, in messianic logic, a refusal of death.

From the very beginning, however, it is clear that Jesus cannot win: He is out of step with respect to *all* the opposing forces. Crowds follow Him for a time on the basis of misunderstandings. It is not enough to say that this strategy is "messianic," that it is "Kingdom" strategy. Belo fails to say *what sort of a strategy it is*. By speaking of Jesus' geographical movements and of subversion of political codes, Belo has not shown how these produce or constitute a strategy! The only genuinely strategic elements Belo mentions, rather vaguely, are Jesus' supposed intention of speaking to the crowds outside the towns, and His clandestine character as implying a movement toward the pagan nations (pp. 154, 156, 211). But what does this mean? That

---

14. Here we have a little example showing how Belo proceeds in the reduction of the text: it deals with the people who carry the paralytic to Jesus and make an opening in the roof of the house. The text reads: "When Jesus saw their faith" (Mark 2:5). Since we must not add to the text, or have preconceived ideas or a ready-made vocabulary, we will say that Jesus sees people carrying a sick man and trying to approach Him: *that* is what He calls "faith." Thus we can say that faith is a little strategy for approaching Jesus' body (see Belo, p. 108). Fine. But I could make this even more precise: Jesus sees these people make a hole in the roof; *that* is what He calls faith. Thus faith is the action of making a hole in a roof!

Jesus had to leave Jewish territory to find support elsewhere? That would amount to a strategy, but in that case, why did He go to Jerusalem and put His head in the lion's mouth?

If Jesus meant to practice total subversion without any sociopolitical support, if He did not attempt to put concrete forces in motion that would enable Him to win, we must not speak of strategy. From the outset, Jesus is inevitably overcome, from the world's point of view. If Jesus imagined for a single moment that He could win, using Belo's famous "strategy," if He thought He could make His adversaries retreat, He was truly stupid! It is absurd to write "The STR [strategy] of Jesus is thus vanquished by the STR of the AA [adversaries]" (p. 217). Neither His mode of action nor its implementation can be reduced to politics. Rather, they constitute a fundamental questioning of all politics.

I can hear the reader retort that Belo emphasizes that Jesus' strategy is that of the *Kingdom*, not merely some Machiavellian calculation! Fine! This means that the "Kingdom" possesses a dimension or quality that remains outside this analysis. Since we are dealing with a *Kingdom* strategy, we see put into play a different "politics," a different behavior and set of actions, with a differing purpose. The Kingdom is not the equivalent of class struggle, a simple revolt against the rich and the occupying force; Lenin showed that class struggle and such revolt are typical of Machiavellian strategy. Thus the Kingdom is not amenable to materialist analysis, since it requires a strategy that seems stupid, from a materialist point of view. When we discover another, irreducible dimension in it, however, it no longer seems stupid.

Belo has clearly misunderstood Jesus' action in the Gospels: it has not been proved that Jesus carried out a *political* struggle in the modern sense of the word. On the contrary, it has been shown that the first generations of Christians interpreted the conflict as political (see John's Apocalypse). This fact ought to diminish the strength of the continually recurring argument that Jesus' successors softened, spiritualized, depoliticized the conflict, etc. From some points of view this is true, but not with regard to politics.

Nevertheless, if Jesus did not carry out a political struggle, He certainly combated societal structure and the destruction of the human being of His time (and of all time!). But His combat did not take place on the level of armed revolution or politics. It was not a matter of power or economic structure: He took His stand at a deeper level, as we will see when we consider the question of anarchism (Chapter VII). Jesus questions *all* economic activity, including what would later be exercised in a socialist world. Consequently He challenged the very foundation of a materialist interpretation of life!

We could say that Belo offers us an ideological discourse on the Gospel, rather than the ideology of the Gospel. But he should have remembered that for Marx a sound ideology is possible only if it is related to sound praxis. And sound praxis remains impossible in a capitalist society.

Throughout his book, Belo replaces knowable reality by a set of images he interprets on an abstract, rather than a theoretical, basis. Furthermore, he eliminates any possibility of debate, declaring with an amazing intransigence that anything that disagrees with his interpretations reeks of bourgeois ideology. In this fashion, with a single word, he brushes aside everything written that fails to line up with his ideology—without engaging in further "scientific" debate. In short, he indulges in a practice common since the beginning of "Christianity": using Jesus and biblical texts to rationalize one's own ideas, choices, and interests, thus falsifying the Gospel.

I find it perfectly respectable for Belo to have chosen politics, the Left, and revolution, since he believes he can serve the poor this way. It follows normally that he should adopt a set of beliefs consistent with that choice. I deny, however, on the one hand, that these choices and beliefs spring from the Gospel, and, on the other hand, that one should use the Gospel to rationalize such choices. Whether Belo likes it or not, the Gospel has another dimension, without which the basic questioning I profoundly believe in (including questioning politics) fails to take place.

8. Conclusion

Let me now conclude this long criticism of Belo's work. I have analyzed his book in detail, not to show that he has failed to ac-

complish his ends, but because this detailed analysis demonstrates that he has come up against obstacles that I believe are
insurmountable. The errors and historical lacunae I criticize are
not accidental: if Belo had known and accepted the facts and the
historical reality as far as we can know them, he would have had
to abandon his theme and his interpretation grid.

A materialist reading can perhaps be applied to some documents, but certainly not to those accounting for an extraordinary phenomenon such as Jesus. In such cases it is essential to
consider the irrational element. How can we explain that the
failure of this insignificant Jewish rebel became the driving force
behind a civilization lasting two thousand years? How can we
explain that among a thousand potential Jesus figures—Jewish
rebels, rebel slaves, ideologues proclaiming a spiritual message,
etc.—this particular one broke through in such a way?

The materialist and historical method should be able to explain this kind of phenomenon; it is not enough to say that materialism explains Jesus' strategy this way or that way: it should
explain why He triumphed where others failed. Until one has
explained this fact, one has merely added another interesting
commentary to the stack of tens of thousands which explain
nothing. It is impossible to discover the meaning of words used
in a text of Jesus' time using only force relations, production
structures, a code *we choose to call* symbolic, or a code *we decide
to call* mythological: this amounts to pseudoscience.

A materialist reading of the Gospel cannot avoid fluttering
between vague, nebulous, and undetermined ideas (giving a
precise impression!) on the one hand, and, on the other, totally
arbitrary assertions concerning the concepts used (in order to
nail such ideas down). These concepts are not defined with respect to reality, which is inaccessible, but with respect to the objective to be attained.

One of the most critical points deals with Belo's omissions.
His reading "discovers" some aspects of the Gospel text (but
these can be, and have been, for the most part, discovered
without his complicated approach). It leaves out an undeniable
dimension of the text, however. As Paul Ricoeur has said, there
is a "surplus of meaning"—and what a surplus!

The materialist method, however, because of the origin of its conception, must be total: it claims to account for everything—otherwise *it fails to be materialist*. It is ultimately impossible, since it would suppose a set of facts and information no one in the world can have. To carry out an effective materialist analysis, one would have to have not merely a summary and superficial idea of forces of production and production relations, but a complete and coherent knowledge (such as the one Marx tries to establish for the working class and the nineteenth-century English economy). But such knowledge is historically impossible. Thus one must fill in for missing knowledge with overall labels or "pseudo-facts" invented out of whole cloth, or with patent distortions of facts we know something of. At this point the reading becomes ideological.

The most one can say, therefore, is that he is attempting a reading with a materialist *intention* and *orientation*—no more. The error lies, then, not in looking for a new means of explanation that would be unencumbered by centuries of accumulated meaning. Nor would it be a mistake to bring the social and economic dimension to bear on interpretation. The error consists of labeling these efforts "materialist," thus giving the undertaking a spectacular, passionate flavor. Furthermore, the word *materialist* has no genuine content in this case, since the author does not provide his ideological presuppositions, which would enable the reader to understand why one should attempt a *materialist* approach.

Thus I consider a "materialist" reading as one possibility among others. It is the expression of its author's commitment. It represents one point of view, but no more scientific or free from ideology than other sorts of readings: symbolic, allegorical, christocentric, critical, structuralist, or a simple, natural reading. But this pseudo-materialist reading becomes strictly ideological (and even idealist) and anti-scientific when it claims to be the only possible approach, seeing itself as exclusive, exhaustive, complete, and able to uncover a meaning in the text that was previously obscured.

Chapter VI

Inductive Theology: The Quest for a Materialist Theology*

Obviously, a materialist reading of the biblical text was not enough. Someone had to try to work out a special theological method, possibly going so far as to formulate a materialist or Marxist theology (the terms "Marxist" and "materialist" often become interchangeable in such studies). Thus we have works of this type by D. Sölle, G. Casalis, J. Cardonnel, G. Girardi, etc. (omitting the Latin American liberation theologies, as we have already mentioned).

Here I will take Casalis's book as my example, since it has pursued research along these lines further than the others.[1] It is difficult to analyze a book that is both coherent and muddled, made up of apparent reasoning interlaced with bursts of enthusiasm. Casalis's book attempts to work out a method.

1. Deductive and Inductive Theology

First we will examine the dispute that became famous in the 1970s: deductive versus inductive theology. Without entering

---

* Sections of this chapter originally appeared in "Les Idées fausses ne tombent pas du ciel," *Réforme*, no. 1741 (5 Aug. 1978), p. 7, as part of Ellul's review of Casalis's book, *Les idées justes ne tombent pas du ciel* (Paris: Les Éditions du Cerf, 1977); Eng. trans. by Sister Jeanne Marie Lyons and Michael John, *Correct Ideas Don't Fall from the Skies: Elements for an Inductive Theology* (Maryknoll, NY: Orbis, 1984).—TRANS.

1. An exception to this is Belo's article "Universalité et contextualité," in *Parole et Société* (1978), a remarkable study of the meaning of the theological and God as image. But of course it also continues to make use of Belo's central ideas of "practice" and of reducing the entire gospel to a messianism of economic practice.

the fray, we might say that deductive theology begins with the recognition of previously established principles or an overall view, and deduces its consequences from that foundation. Inductive theology steers clear of principles, places itself in an incongruous universe, proceeds on the basis of trial and error, and progressively, by induction, searches for a possible coherence and generalization.

For example, in one kind of deductive theology, the Bible is considered a given,[2] and one draws consequences from it, such as in ethics. Another sort of deduction begins with spiritual or religious experience, a life experience of revelation, etc., and by means of these experiences, one arrives progressively at a deeper understanding of the biblical revelation. This approach has been confirmed by many recent historical works, showing that the biblical texts did not always fall in their present form from the Holy Spirit's mouth. They were not God-breathed in that sense, but rather slowly developed as an interpretation of the revelation, over a period of generations.

A. Social Class

After this beginning, we move on with Casalis to a second stage: thought is narrowly defined and determined by experience. In other words, we clearly live first and think afterward, in terms of what we live. At this point, of course, Casalis inserts Marxism; the principle of "live first, think afterward" constitutes one aspect of materialism. This idea clearly goes beyond the overused quotation (not from Marx): "thought is secreted by the brain just as bile is produced by the liver." Marx's view was never so simple.

Materialism amounts essentially to the affirmation that the phenomena of consciousness appear after the phenomena of material existence. Material existence, for a human being, is always social life, since Marx says that work characterizes it.

---

2. Quite often in this method biblical texts are made into "principles," a practice I completely rejected as early as my *Présence au monde moderne* (Geneva: Roulet, 1948) (Eng. trans. by Olive Wyon, *The Presence of the Kingdom* [Philadelphia: Westminster; London: SCM, 1951; repr. New York: Seabury, 1967]).

Thought is thus produced by work, and by the instruments, relations, and organization of work. If work becomes alienated, thought produces an ideology. And since the alienation of work brings class division with it, thought is determined by one's class. In fact, one's class determines the nature of all action or practice.

Belonging to a social class defines our life, and the only practice we must take into account is our political practice in the class struggle. From this perspective, theology does not come from God and does not express eternal truth for a given time. Furthermore, theology is an ideology that depends on my connection with a given social class. Like all ideologies, its goal is to rationalize and legitimize the class I belong to: the ruling class, of course.

In other words, as Casalis shows clearly, no deductive theology exists, since biblical principles are chosen in terms of the ruling class's practice. Biblical interpretation and theological formulation are deduced from the Bible in a fallacious manner. In reality, such interpretations and formulations express the ruling class's situation and are arrived at inductively from its practice. All theology is inductive, in the sense that it is preceded by a practice determined by our class; our way of being and acting depends on the class to which we belong. A Christian is characterized by his choice of class, which results from his imitation of Jesus. Jesus also found Himself in a class situation, and He placed Himself resolutely in the class of the poor and alienated.

Based on this practice stemming from our identification with the poor, theology, or the task of reflecting on this practice, consists first of all of gathering the facts related to the experience of class struggle. Then one must organize this material, thus creating a new (inductive) theology, consistent with Jesus' teaching, since His teaching was the expression of His commitment. Thus, to have a good, true theology, one must be on Jesus' side. Jesus was on the side of the poor, and everything He taught resulted from that practice. Taking the side of the poor, oppressed, and exploited, then, means having the same practice as Jesus. Taking their side means placing oneself where one can truly understand what Jesus said. And a theology can be arrived at inductively from this practice (a theology of revolution, liberation, etc.). I believe this to be Casalis's point of departure.

Two questions arise immediately, however: (1) The theology Casalis presents to us most certainly does not rest on ready-made biblical, religious, or Christian ideas from the past. But does it really rest on practice? Isn't there a set of ready-made ideas and a priori ideas behind it? (2) What practice is involved, then?

With respect to the first question, when one reads Casalis carefully, it becomes quite clear that he posits a certain number of principles (never explicit or demonstrated) from which everything else is deduced. These are utterly hidden, perhaps unconsciously, all traces of them having been removed, so that they appear as intangible givens that are obvious and cannot be criticized. Following the thread of these principles in Casalis's book, one can assemble a sort of creed or implicit decalogue:

1. Marx is always right and Marxism is a science. The obviously scientific nature of Marxism need not be demonstrated (Marx is the last word on everything for Casalis; amazingly enough, however, even Marxist intellectuals hesitate to proclaim the scientific value of Marxism).[3]

2. Politics first: a person's sincerity is judged on the basis of his political practice (in the class struggle).

3. Class struggle is a scientific truth:[4] the fundamental reality. It enables us to understand and explain everything. Casalis never defines "class," of course, and he improperly transforms the struggle of the oppressed, the poor, etc., into a class struggle in the precise Marxist sense of the term. We have here an intel-

---

3. When Geoltrain disagrees with A. Dumas and claims Casalis has not "canonized" Marxism, I feel he has read Casalis's book rather hurriedly and has picked up only its overall ideas. As Dumas says, this canonization appears on every page, and is by no means limited to class struggle (to which Geoltrain limits his response). Instead, Casalis's canonization of Marxism involves all the principles of Marx's thought, especially in that his thought is considered the criterion for the true interpretation of the modern world.

4. In a remarkable way, Ellenstein declares that when Marxism calls itself scientific, it becomes ideological (Le Matin, 4 Oct. 1978).

lectual orientation that must lead those who take the side of the poor into the Marxist system.

4. Socialism is the expression of the poor and oppressed; the Communist parties truly defend their interests. The triumph of socialism is their triumph (here Casalis identifies the poor with socialism).

5. The revolution must be socialist, and on Marx's terms. Any idea of some other type of revolution is necessarily counterrevolutionary.

6. We must not speak of present socialist regimes or confront Marxism's internal and obligatory logic with the Gulag (undoubtedly errors have been committed, but we must not take them into account, since in any case the poor are those who . . . , etc.).

7. The revolution is always right and revolutionary action is always exemplary. Thus we must never question it for theological reasons. A theology that called the revolution into question would be counterrevolutionary.

8. The people (that is, the oppressed) are always right, spontaneously.

9. Only a militant can understand what Jesus says, since only he has a (revolutionary) praxis. There can be only one class of militants: the socialist-Communist type.

10. It does not matter at all whether we recognize and confess Jesus explicitly as the Christ, since all that matters is a practice in accord with Jesus' practice.[5]

---

5. Concerning Jesus' practice, many authors try to make Him a revolutionary leader, but this no longer suffices: He must also be a *class* partisan. He placed Himself at the head of the alienated class. Naturally, if he is to justify such an interpretation, an author must resolutely force many texts and select only those that could conceivably allude to such an idea. The rest are discreetly discarded, called later additions by a Church (undoubtedly beginning with the first generation!) that took the side of the exploiting class and transformed the record of Jesus' practice. But in taking such a position one would have at the very least to grapple with the following question: if Jesus' disciples were the best representatives of the oppressed class, why did they distort their leader's practice to such a point, beginning at the time of His death? Or, if they had already been won over by the exploiting class, in what sense can we call Jesus a leader of the oppressed class?

These are the fundamental, undeclared (much less demonstrated) principles from which Casalis's whole argument develops. Obviously, each of the items in this creed can be fundamentally challenged, since they are clearly out of line! But I will point out only two of their consequences: (1) Casalis's theology is *deductive*. He claims that "classical" theology, whether Augustine, Thomas Aquinas, Luther, or Calvin, is necessarily inductive, since it is arrived at inductively from the theologian's membership in the ruling class. Classical theology, according to Casalis, reflects the ideas of the ruling class, and then covers itself over with a blanket of biblical precepts. With these precepts the theologian claims to arrive at his theology by deduction, when in fact the theology was already given.

But if a person's class practice is good (that is, if he belongs to the oppressed), says Casalis, he can move from it to true theology: the theology of the rediscovery of Jesus' practice. But this is all mere illusion. We must turn the situation around: in reality Casalis merely substitutes Marxist principles (or pseudo- or para-Marxist principles!) for biblical principles and then proceeds deductively!

(2) With this so-called inductive theology, we find ourselves quite simply in the presence of a resurgence of natural theology—nothing else. It has merely changed its frame of reference. When human life was lived mainly in nature's environment, the main preoccupation was nature the invader, and human nature was the central matter to be resolved. At that time people were greatly tempted to derive their theology from nature, or at least to harmonize Christian theology and nature's laws or imperatives.

The situation has changed, however; society has become the human environment: the invasion of our lives and their limitations now come from the social milieu, and human beings are conceived primarily as social beings, a set of relationships, etc. Now, then, our social condition has become the essential factor—based on natural evidence, of course! At this point, the temptation (like the earlier one, but now with a new object) involves deriving theology from society, from a person's place in society and his social condition. This amounts to exactly the same adulteration of revealed truth.

Praxis theology entails all the features of natural theology and leads to the same syncretisms, along with some additional ones. Although the syncretisms are the same, they deal with different themes. Traditionally, syncretism resulted from the religion of nature, whereas today we find its themes result from the religion of society. But the so-called a-religious Christianity that some try to offer is a-religious only with respect to the ancient religious forms. It is totally religious as far as politics, revolution, economic growth, happiness, socioeconomic equality, decolonization, etc., are concerned.[6]

Finally, I would like to try to straighten out a misunderstanding. With my first published books, in the late 1940s (and at the same time, in a methodology notebook Jean Bosc and I prepared for the Protestant Professional Associations in France), I established the principle of tension between life experience and revelation. We can grasp revelation, accepted as a given, only through interpretations, of course, but it remains independent of our interpretations. These involve our thought processes, but thinking is not merely a translation of our life experience. Naturally, thought results from the cultural framework within which it is expressed, from the very forms it uses in its processes, from its sets of understandings, etc. But in the case of revelation as a given, thought finds itself face to face with an indomitable reality which contradicts everything cultural, if we take revelation seriously. This is precisely what all the biblical texts teach us, the Prophets and the Epistles as well as the Gospels: as revelation they offer a fundamental challenge to *everything* cultural, social, and political in a given society. They even challenge the challengers.

Revelation truly comes "from heaven,"[7] since "My thoughts are not your thoughts" (Isa. 55:8). This has nothing to do with any practice whatever. Rather, it is truly the thought of the Wholly Other, which does not result from any human activity. Every attempt to be faithful to this revelation produces the same

---

6. See my *The New Demons*, trans. C. Edward Hopkin (New York: Seabury, 1975).

7. *Ciel*, the same word translated as "skies" in the title of Casalis's book.—TRANS.

contradiction (which is in no way social or economic!). As soon as reconciliation occurs, we should become suspicious, even if reconciliation with a rebel trend takes place. The quest to reconcile Marxism and Christianity is just like all the others that have taken place throughout history.

In summary, then, we have confrontation between what is experienced, on the one hand, and what is "thought in revelation," on the other. But we must continually go back and begin again with what is "thought in revelation." Thus we must involve ourselves in rereading the biblical texts, based on the challenge of our experience and practice. And we must also involve ourselves in precisely the opposite activity: challenging experience, facts, and practice, based on the revelation as known and understood on its own terms. No simple method exists: we cannot begin with praxis in order to discover correct ideas, nor can we begin with ready-made ideas coming directly from heaven that could tell us clearly what to do.[8]

In other words, there can be neither inductive nor deductive theology: both are false. We must repeatedly begin the confrontation afresh, if revelation is to be incarnate (as, for example, when an ethic results from understanding the Scriptures), and if life experience is to be expressed (rather than repressed; for example, the understanding of Scripture should come about in the light of experience *also*, but not only in its light).

This permanent contradiction, this approach that makes its way through confrontation, is the only genuinely dialectical approach. But it does not exclude—on the contrary, it presupposes—that the revealed "given" is really given by the Transcendent One, and that the Holy Spirit constitutes the effective link between each of us and the biblical text. The earthbound circle of praxis and theory excludes the Holy Spirit, of course, and presupposes that one can speak of God apart from any revelation, based only on experience. This view appears to me doubly to contradict scriptural teaching, however it may be interpreted.

---

8. A group of us have tried to express this confrontational approach involving life and revelation, experience and theology, in our proposed reform of Protestant theological studies. But we never suggested an inductive theological approach in Casalis's sense.

B. Class Struggle

Now we arrive at the second issue: so-called inductive theology is based on praxis; good theology is based on the praxis of class struggle in favor of the oppressed. Here our problem becomes a double one: (1) What does it mean to be "in favor of" the oppressed? (2) What praxis is involved?

The answer to the first question involves the intriguing idea of "ideological belonging." Christianity, as it has been understood until now, is nothing but a theo-ideology, the expression of a false conscience and the justification of a ruling class, according to Casalis. In other words, Christianity is not the proclamation of truth, the quest for a form of life, the experience (among other things) of a transcendence, the discovery of a new way of being. This is all simple illusion, since it can only be attributed to one's class situation.

It is simple illusion, for example, to believe that you can escape from your class through Christianity! You belong either to the class of the oppressed or to the oppressors. Fine. But, of course, this all changes when conversion to the proletariat is involved! An admirable about-face (not found in Marx) enables a person to move from a class "situation" to a chosen class "position." A member of the proletariat finds himself in a class situation, as an oppressed person. But the bourgeois who, *ideologically* (since it never happens any other way), chooses to be in the proletarian camp (without entering their situation) does exactly what he must in order to be on the good side! *That* is conversion.

Who can make us believe that such a person thus becomes oppressed, exploited, a creator of merchandise, etc.? When Casalis has the audacity to write that the popular "masses" accepted Marx into their ranks (p. 26), this proves that he is unacquainted with the facts and gets carried away by his imagination. The entire debate between Marx and Bakunin centered on this point. Bakunin at least respected the proletariat and knew that he had no right to head its revolution! But all the bourgeois intellectuals who have claimed this "conversion" take another tack.

In summary, the ideological movement that promotes class politics (that is, Marxist revolutionary action) provides its adherents with the label "proletarian" (and therefore "Christian," since the only proof of our Christianity is that we rally to the cause of the poor). But the ideological movement that expresses an encounter with God, irrespective of one's class relation, has no meaning.

Finally, we must understand that the important issue if one wishes to belong to the proletariat is heartfelt identification with the cause (and involvement in a praxis, as we shall see), in Casalis's view. Thus the proletariat is composed, on the one hand, of those who suffer the proletarian condition (alienation, work as merchandise, which produces added value), and, on the other hand, of those who suffer nothing of all this, but whose heart is with the proletariat ("Courage, workers!," as Fellini's Vitelloni said).

I realize that this conclusion may shock those who believe they have entered the proletarian struggle; but for Marx this struggle can only spring from the condition in which one finds oneself. We must be careful in our reasoning: either one believes that socioeconomic conditions effectively determine praxis and the phenomena of conscience, in which case one is a consistent materialist (but this means a bourgeois can never have the praxis of a member of the proletariat). Or else one believes that an ideological choice determines people's praxis, in which case one is not a materialist.

The answer to our second question (concerning what praxis is involved) proves that in reality this "conversion" to the proletariat is always limited to an inclination of the heart. What do these theologians of materialist theology actually *do*?

Let's leave out the few Latin American priests who courageously joined guerrilla forces, and in some cases paid for this decision with their lives. "Leave them out?" you say, "but they are the best examples we have." Be careful! If you think that way, you must stop judging the Church on the basis of socioeconomic reality, and judge it only on the basis of its martyrs! If we refuse to do this, and prefer to judge the Church on the basis of its usual praxis, then we must look not at the three or four martyrs of liberation theology, but at the general body of Marxist Christians and their praxis (in any case, from the Marxist point of view, there is no *individual exemplarity* in social praxis!).

What, then, is the concrete, genuine praxis of Marxist Christians? They are all intellectuals. What allows them to say you can understand the gospel only on the basis of a practice of class struggle? How can they proclaim this practice except as an idea (which has no more value than any other)? After all, praxis cannot be reduced to the fact that one has sided with the poor, or to a declaration that one is for them!

What, then, is the praxis of Marxist Christians? As far as I can tell, their practice consists of giving lectures, writing articles, traveling to congresses and colloquia, attending demonstrations, signing petitions and manifestos, and organizing seminars. They may sometimes participate in a parade with raised fist, meet with militants of the far Left, or make "revolutionary" statements. But I contend, on the one hand, that this behavior involves no praxis, and, on the other hand, that the same act done by a Marxist Christian and by a member of the proletariat has a different meaning.

First, such actions do not amount to praxis. Praxis entails commitment to a transformation of social relationships. This transformation will not come about through demonstrations in which any intellectual can participate. This is all the more true because praxis cannot be separated from the exercise of an economically situated profession. To the degree that Marxist Christians' verbally revolutionary activities have nothing in common with their profession, to the degree that they continue to be bourgeois professors, lawyers, pastors, or Dominicans, we cannot consider their actions as praxis.[9]

Second, the same act accomplished by one of these honorable partisans and by a member of the proletariat is in no way comparable. For the member of the proletariat, there is no distance between his work and the strike or popular demonstra-

---

9. Extreme confusion exists in this regard. Geoltrain (in *Réforme*, April 1978) was able to write that "Casalis speaks on the basis of a practice within conflicts that divide societies on an international level, and he expresses this practice in terms of class struggle." But Casalis merely *speaks on the basis of his opinions* and convictions (like everybody else), which have led him to join (doctrinally) a political movement. But this in no way amounts to speaking on the basis of a practice, since only others' practice is involved.

tion in which he participates: when he engages in such action, his life is on the line. He wants to change his future, his own existence. In the other case, however, we have mere intellectual pleasure. If the strike fails, the consequences for the worker will be grave. For the Marxist Christian, the only consequence is his disappointment.

Marxist Christians say that they have taken up the cause of the poor, Marxism, and the revolution, but any committed intellectual does the same thing. Such commitment is purely verbal, rather than a revolutionary practice. It amounts even less to "praxis" in Marx's sense, since these people have no contact with reality. They do not work with their hands, under the orders of a boss, in miserable living and working conditions.

We must not forget that for Marx the revolutionary factor is *being* a proletarian rather than *thinking* a certain way. Others are merely in contact with an imaginary reality or a hallucination. A conference, even if revolutionary, does not amount to reality in Marx's sense. For this reason, these Marxist-Christian intellectuals make as serious a mistake as in 1945-48 (the comparison is not too farfetched). At that time many of our Marxist Christians championed Stalin and Stalinism so faithfully that not even the 20th Congress or the ghastly experience of Hungary could make them wince. How many times did I hear one of them mouth the usual slogans: "Even if concentration camps exist in the Soviet Union, it remains the home of socialism and the true revolution. The Soviet camps have nothing in common with Hitler's, and Soviet dictatorship has nothing in common with Nazi totalitarianism. The important thing is the Soviet regime's purpose: justice and the victory of the poor, of course. We must not criticize the Soviet Union; that just plays into the hands of the reactionaries. We must accompany the Communists as they make their way." Those who declare themselves Marxist Christians today used to repeat such talk endlessly.

For me it is a serious matter that Marxist-Christian theologians redouble their efforts precisely when almost all Marxist intellectuals look with horror on their error and wonder how they could have been so mistaken. Our theologians who were "Stalin's fellow travelers" fail to make even a vague effort at self-criticism. They hang onto their clear, unruffled conscience,

forgetting that unfortunate time and continuing to preach
Marxism as if nothing had happened. Their ability to carry on
in this manner shows they have never had a true experience of
praxis. Their error and their lapse of memory show that they
have never had any revolutionary or proletarian practice. Naturally, they cannot criticize a praxis they never had!

These theologians *talk about* practice rather than *living* it.
Consequently they cannot develop a theology related to their
praxis. Talking about *others'* practice has no purpose, even if a
genuine practice is involved. From the Marxist point of view,
you can think and develop a conscience free from falsification
only based on your *own* practice and beginning from there.
Otherwise, obviously, any bourgeois intellectual could *recount*
workers' practice and avoid a false conscience on that basis. But
Marx categorically rejects this possibility.

If our Marxist theologians have no experience of praxis
(apart from mere ideas!), what gives them the right to declare
that nothing but revolutionary praxis, nothing but a "classist"
reading enables a person to understand the Gospels and to read
the Bible correctly? Such statements amount to mere rhetoric.
Let's get serious: as far as Marx is concerned, either you have a
revolutionary practice, which enables you to have an ideology-
free conscience, or you do not have it, in which case your conscience remains distorted.

Casalis understands correctly that one must base a philosophical system on workers' praxis, if one wishes to follow Marx.
The philosophy is fulfilled in the proletarian revolution, and the
proletarian revolution is fulfilled in the philosophy. Thus we can
say the same for theology: a materialist theology is possible only
if rooted in praxis. But then, obviously, such a praxis must exist.
For although one can refer to proletarian praxis in general when
establishing a materialist philosophy, for a materialist theology
one would have the right to refer only to the proletarian praxis
of *Christians*. And in no way can one refer to Jesus' praxis, since,
as we have seen, (1) no proletariat was involved; (2) the interpretation of Jesus as having had a revolutionary practice in the
modern sense depends on a series of wordplays and forcing of
the text; (3) no one could begin claiming Jesus had a revolutionary praxis until the time when the ideology of Marxist revolution

became part of our thinking. In other words, *this* Jesus is discovered not on the basis of what He is, but on the basis of a presupposition acquired from one's social milieu.

We must finally come to the point where we ask this question: What does *good* praxis involve? Who can choose it? Until 1954, Stalin's praxis was held to be unquestionably good. After the "Khrushchev Report," however, Stalin's praxis was no longer considered good. What about Mao? Now we learn that his praxis must be completely revised. Best of all, no one says we should stop imitating their practice because circumstances have changed. No: a retroactive decision is involved. We are told Stalin was never a Communist! We had already heard this from Lenin when he ran Kautsky down, and from Stalin when he shot down N. Bukharin. Both were said to have erred in their praxis *from the outset*.

You think, then, that you can select the right praxis? The formula "practice is the only criterion of truth" amounts to a farce, since a thousand possible practices exist, and no definitive criterion for choosing among them. You think you have the definitive criterion: supporting and helping the poor? Then you will have to break quickly with Communism, since *its practice* has produced many more radically poor people than capitalism ever did. Communism has never defended the truly poor: only those who were useful to the revolution.

This is not merely my opinion; the founders to a man affirm the same thing: Marx was first to declare that poor peasants, beggars, destitute old people, and those on the fringes of society held no interest. Lenin likewise: for him, colonized peoples never amounted to anything but a "reserve" for the proletariat. "Well," you ask, "how about the poor in themselves, for their own sake?" Whenever Communism takes the form of Marxism and becomes a Party bent on the conquest of power, it could not care less about the poor.

C. Inductive Theology and Christian Faith

At this point we must ask a final question: Can we conceive of this sort of inductive theology from the point of view of faith in Jesus Christ? In reality this inductive theology, built on the lines of Marx's "theory-practice" model, rests on a series of misun-

derstandings. It involves not only, as we have seen, an erroneous identification of evangelical practice with Marxist
praxis, but also an erroneous identification of the revealed Word
with ideas and theory. Marx always vigorously denied that
theory could be reduced to ideas. Theory is a strictly scientific
construction. Never is it the same as more or less precise or coherent ideas. Theory must be constantly revised by practice.
Ideas have no importance in Marx.

"In this sense," someone will say, "theology is of course a
kind of theory." I accept this formulation, if the theory is scientific. But theology as theory cannot have its source and ground
in practice alone, since it rests on another factor Marx cannot
take into account: revelation by the Word of God. As Christians
we must take this factor into account.

Shall we say Jesus' word amounts to nothing but the expression of His practice? Note first of all that from Marx's perspective, Jesus never gives us a scientific theory, but rather a proclamation or a commandment. We cannot equate these with a
theory. Next, note that Jesus by His word sometimes indeed expresses what He does, by way of explanation; but how can we
deny that He had a completely different source of inspiration in
the Torah and the Prophets? In them He refers not to a practice
but to a word from the past, which He accepts as is. Jesus affirms
still another source of inspiration that we would have some difficulty depriving Him of: the direct inspiration coming from
God His Father, in prayer and communion with Him. It is
strictly impossible to eliminate this factor (unless we destroy the
Gospels!) and reduce all Jesus' "teaching" to the explanation of
His practice. We may do theology, but Jesus did not. We can say
our theology should be the expression of our practice, but this
implies eliminating Jesus' word as our main authoritative
source. Can we call such a theology "Christian"?

Furthermore, this so-called inductive theology runs counter
to the clearest biblical texts. Consider the structure of Paul's
Epistles; we all know they tend to have two parts: first, teaching concerning the revelation of God in Jesus, the Good News
concerning Jesus. Second, as a consequence of the first part, we
find a description of a practice that should flow out from the
teaching (as in the famous "Therefore" of Rom. 12:1). The prac-

tice comes as a result (and not as the point of departure) of Paul's theology of Jesus and the gospel. The only way out of this dilemma is to accept the idea that Paul was mistaken, a really poor theologian who was unable to take Marx's courses on what good theology should be.

We cannot expect to find a solution to this problem by suggesting that Paul builds his theology on the basis of his previous experience (the road to Damascus, for example). From Marx's perspective, experience is not the same thing as praxis. In any case, Paul insists that what he says is not based on his subjective experiences: he sets them aside so as not to detract from the objective revelation he received. But let's set Paul aside, since in any case he has received bad press from the new theological trends.

We must, however, deal with Jesus' explicit words. I will select two examples dealing with the matter of "putting into practice": (1) the well-known parable of the house built on sand (Matt. 7:24-27); and (2) Jesus' answer to the Pharisees who asked Him to prove His word was true (John 7:17).

(1) The parable has as its outline: "Every one then who hears these words of mine and does them. . . . And every one who hears these words of mine and does not do them . . ." (Matt. 7:24, 26). Some would react then by saying that putting into practice is the key to everything, since this determines whether the house stands or falls. But in reality we see, on the contrary, that the first issue is listening to the Word. The outline is not: act, develop the theory of this action, and then rectify the action. Rather, it is: listen to this word (which does not go beyond "these words *of mine*"; it is not even a question of "do as I do"!), and *then* decide if you will put this word into practice. Putting into practice here has as its basis *listening* and faith in the validity of the *person* of Jesus ("these words of *mine*"). Thus what matters is a practice in accordance with Jesus' teaching, rather than a practice on which a Christian theory may be constructed. And Jesus' teaching in this Sermon on the Mount in no way regards class struggle or social justice, etc. The Word spoken by God and transmitted by Jesus precedes: it transmits a truth that comes *before* all practice and action. It *gives rise to* the practice, but exists at the outset.

(2) The statement in John 7:17 is even more significant: "If anyone wills to do His will (the will of Him who sent me), he will know if my doctrine is from God or if I speak on my own account."[10] Very clearly, then, there is a "doing" that permits a "knowing," where "doctrine" is concerned. This point is extremely important for our discussion. But what is one to "do"? God's will. This revealed will exists before our practice. By executing this will, we can discern if Jesus' teaching is true. This implies that by accomplishing (putting into practice) the will of God, we discover the agreement between Jesus' teaching and what God demands.

Such putting into practice enables us to discern the truth, not of a practice, but of a teaching. To me this seems consistent with overall biblical teaching: doing enables one to know the truth of the Word; it gives access to its complete meaning. But what does one discover according to this text? Whether my doctrine is *mine* or *from God!* In other words, Jesus' teaching, His doctrine, is in no way the theory of His practice. Rather it is the expression of what God has revealed to Him. From the outset, *God's* decision governs all doctrine, all teaching; putting into practice is merely a test enabling us to understand and penetrate a revelation that has nothing to do with the inference of a practice. Marx's "think as you act" is radically false as far as the Bible is concerned, even if it is partially correct in sociological terms.

In conclusion, we should remember the great proclamation: "For my thoughts are not your thoughts, neither are your ways my ways" (Isa. 55:8). In the face of this radical judgment, how could we infer something true, something in accordance with the gospel, on the basis of human practice? All human practice is erroneous. All human thought is deceitful. Correct thoughts and practices are found in God and come from Him. Whatever one's practice may be, if one infers a theology from it, it will be a theology of lies. The only foundation possible is the revelation of "what no eye has seen, nor ear heard, nor the heart of man conceived" (1 Cor. 2:9). On this basis, which we are obliged to consider as something given in advance, we must elaborate a theology in our present situation, and *also* one related to our

---

10. Ellul's own translation.—TRANS.

ability to live out what the gospel requires. For this reason theology must always be redone.

Theology's basic foundation, however, cannot be the practice of the Christian life; still less can it be a political or class practice. These are always entirely "your practices": human practices that are strictly contradictory to the divine practice, even when they claim to imitate it. The practice of "being with the poor because Jesus became poor" has no more basis than the earlier practice of "being with the powerful because God is All-Powerful"! The difference, of course, is that "being with the poor" represents our present-day conviction, so that it appears unquestionable. In that light my parallel of "being with the powerful" is bound to seem scandalous!

God's power, however, was not the power of kings, and Jesus' poverty is not the poverty of immigrant workers—and when inverted these phrases are even less true! "Your practice is not my practice." For this reason, no inductive theology starting with experience or practice is possible. Such a theology necessarily falsifies. Practice is and should be the critical touchstone of theology. But nothing more.

2. The Uniqueness of Faith

It goes without saying today that the Christian should be a servant of others and on the side of the poor (this actually represents a profound present-day rediscovery, but only with respect to the nineteenth century, since the Church has always had this orientation *among others:* only a wicked lie would claim that the Church amounted to nothing more than its official, Constantinian aspect). It also goes without saying today that in this service and "defense," cooperation between Christians and non-Christians is normal and should be multiplied. Marxist Christians did not invent these two ideas.

The Marxist-Christians' position becomes unacceptable, however, when they claim that only social practice enables a person to understand the Word of God. On the one hand, I never see, in connection with this cooperation with non-Christians, that the latter come to recognize and confess Jesus as Lord (and at this point I remain utterly uncompromising: confessing with the mouth and faith in the heart are the decisive issues). Their praxis in no way enables them to discover that Jesus is the Christ. On the other hand, if a praxis gives birth to an ideology or to a certain form of understanding, it seems elementary to me that participating in the same praxis should give birth to the same knowledge and the same understanding of reality. This was one of the Marxists' presuppositions; and it was painful for them to discover that people with the same praxis could hold to radically opposing theories and doctrines!

We are told that Christians and non-Christians, indifferently mingled, participate in the same revolutionary social practice. If the practice enables one to understand Christianity, it should produce the same explanation in all participants. But the result is altogether different. In Christians there is a dimension that utterly escapes other people: the dimension of faith, the recognition of Jesus as the Christ. This dimension in no way depends on practice: rather, it precedes practice. Faith, rather than praxis, is primary.

Let's try to see if we can avoid misunderstanding: obviously I do not base my argument on the simplistic idea that praxis itself should lead the non-Christian to become a Christian! I mean, rather, that the distance between faith and non-faith is such that the practice in the two cases cannot be identical. If the Christian adopts exactly the same praxis as a non-Christian, this signifies that he has abandoned the primary quality of his faith; he has entered a non-Christian process, putting the poor and their economic interests ahead of the Poor One, and putting a political kingdom ahead of seeking the Kingdom of God. Such complete identification is completely misleading.

By identifying the poor with the Poor One, and a political kingdom with God's Kingdom, the Christian abandons what is specific in Christianity.[11] And if Christianity loses its specificity, there is absolutely no point in continuing to speak of Christianity and Jesus Christ. Political and social commitment can only be something derived from faith—a consequence of it, a way of living it. But if this faith is unique, it necessarily involves

---

11. See my article, "Théologie dogmatique et spécificité du christianisme," *Foi et Vie,* 70, nos. 2-4 (avril-sept. 1971), 139-54.

a different way of living, committing oneself, and being militant. Militancy does not enable me to discover the true knowledge of the revelation; but a personal relationship with the Lord can commit me to militancy.

A. The Basis of Revolution

Here we must face an incredibly difficult question. We see clearly all the evil resulting from capitalist and bourgeois domination. And, to be sure, revolutionary intention seems negatively based: it says no to this world of oppression and alienation. What is revolution *in favor of?* Casalis tells us it is not on behalf of the gospel, or because a person is a Christian, that he should be a revolutionary. What, then? On behalf of Marxism: Marxism as a science that illuminates and explains everything.

Marxism is not a science, however, and above all, it teaches us that everything depends on praxis. Consequently, what is the Communist Party's praxis in Communist countries? What do we see that could convince us to enlist? Tactics based on violence, lies, slavery, and stripping people of everything. We see conquering nations, more nationalistic and imperialistic than the bourgeois nations were. The Communist nations are also more militaristic; they develop their repressive system beyond all limits. They create a new proletariat, failing to grant even the liberties guaranteed (in part) by bourgeois governments. We see societies that are *all* infinitely more bureaucratic and hierarchical than Western societies.

What are we to conclude? On what basis should we arrive at a position of confidence in a hypothetical Communist regime that has never incarnated itself in anything but dictatorships? Are we supposed to commit ourselves to an alliance between Christians and Marxists on this basis? Or develop a political-materialist rereading of the Bible? We would have to be crazy! The insanity here lies in moving from identification with the Poor One to identification with Marxism, and in refusing to consider Marxism as anything but an ideal and a science, whereas in truth it is nothing but a praxis connected with a theory. What we have just seen of Marxist praxis shows the theory to be erroneous.

Casalis, who has been entranced (no other word will do) by

Marxism and converted by the Holy Spirit outpouring of the May 1968 "revolution" in Paris, has become utterly unable to understand these matters. This inability, clearly expressed, has become a voluntary blindness: he explains at one point that one must "look with a prophetic eye at the world we are to reconstruct" (but these words contain absolutely nothing Marxist; they amount to a "Christian" formula Casalis uses to make his other ideas acceptable, and to make the reader forget what the real Marxist world amounts to—there is nothing prophetic about it!).

At another point, in lovely concession, Casalis proclaims: "There is no doubt that a revolution is not going to set everything right, . . . but . . . one day at a time" (p. 76). Thus we should commit ourselves to the Communist revolution, and our children or grandchildren will have to shake off a regime we produced. We have heard this story before: one, two, or three generations must be sacrificed to bring about the certainty of a smiling future! But Casalis sanctimoniously covers over this statement with a saying of Jesus![12] The worst bourgeois theologians proceeded in just this fashion; they had their own certainties, concerning the future of capitalism: happiness, justice, and freedom.

Marxist Christians should learn that they have no right to apply to politics Jesus' words given as the expression of personal faith in the God one trusts. When they use Jesus' words politically, Marxist Christians show how little they have understood of political reality. But Casalis has a defense for what I have just said, since he recognizes that "the path of socialism has been deeply marked with . . . errors," and that "even if socialism . . . had accumulated as many enormities and monstrosities as Christianity has committed during two thousand years, there would be no reason to condemn the one or the other" (p. 179). He also says that "maintaining the status quo offers little save death and burial" (p. 179), whereas revolution represents a risk, but holds out hope as well.

---

12. The quotation of Casalis given above, from the English translation of his book, obscures the biblical allusion (cf. Matt. 6:34) that is present in the original French text.—TRANS.

I agree with him on this last point, as long as the revolution is non-Communist and non-Marxist! We now know, having gone back from Stalin to Lenin and from Lenin to Marx, what we can expect from a Marxist revolution: nothing but what happened in the Soviet Union. If, as some say, something different is happening in Cuba or Angola, this is because their revolution is not Marxist-Communist!

You want a revolution? Which one? And what will it depend on? Simplistically, some answer: "a revolution of the poor." But those who use such language are careful not to let on what they mean! Let's consider the first two of Casalis's three statements quoted above. They sound terrible for a theologian! They actually signify the exclusion of the Transcendent One, the Wholly Other, the God of Abraham, Isaac, Jacob, and Jesus Christ. For Casalis identifies two movements with each other: socialism and Christianity. One is as good as the other. And that would be precisely true: if Jesus were not the Son of the Eternal Creator and Lord, Christianity would have no value. If there is no Transcendent One, beyond history, we have no more reason to hope than if we were throwing dice or playing poker.

Furthermore, I would say that the other presupposition behind this assimilation of Christianity and socialism is that history, as decoded by Marx, is the true god! Socialism's real error, the one that lies behind all the rest, is that it ended up formulating a new *religion*, setting up gods: History, Proletariat, Socialism, Revolution. For only to gods could a person offer holocausts as fearsome as those that have been dedicated to these idols.

B. Marxist Terms in a Christian Context

Marxist Christians always start out with a traditional Christian idea and allow it to be absorbed by socialist idealism. Then, proceeding retroactively, they claim to rediscover this idea thanks to socialism and Marxism. Thus we find Casalis writing: "an authentic revolution aims at the emergence (collective and individual) of a *new human being*" (p. 6). Yes, certainly! Except that I have no way of knowing what an "authentic" revolution might be, judging from what he says.

Let's look at this formula the other way around, however,

beginning with "the emergence (collective and individual) of a new human being." This formulation enables me to erase in one stroke every sort of revolution we have witnessed until the present. Because never, anywhere, has there been such an emergence—not even the beginning of emergence or a hint of a truly new human being. We have seen new regimes and new oppressors, new ruling classes and new institutions, new economic structures and new moralities. But a new human being? Nowhere: not in the Soviet Union, not in Germany (yes, that's right, Germany: Hitler also said that the birth of a new humanity distinguished the Nazi revolution), not in China, Vietnam, Cambodia, or Cuba. Certainly not.

Marxism prepares a new humanity less than any other revolution. For it merely goes back to the humanity of the industrial world, inverting certain structures—nothing else. No revolution based on the principles, praxis, and theory of Marxism can bring about a new humanity, because such a revolution depends on two nineteenth-century presuppositions: work as the supreme value, and progress as the meaning of history.

I would be tempted to laugh bitterly at the idea of a new humanity born out of Marxism, if it were not for all the blood and horror involved in trying to give birth to it. Why laugh? Because this new humanity looks old-fashioned and rather kitschy. I say this because of the concept of morality, family, art, and social relations we see in the Soviet Union. Consistently, these concepts mirror images of Western bourgeois nineteenth-century morality, family, and art.

We can go even further afield: have a good look at Liu Ch'ao-Chi's remarkable little book, *Being a Good Communist*, the Bible of the Chinese revolution before Mao's little *Red Book* (Liu's book is on the verge of replacing Mao's again). Any good liberal Protestant reading this book of morals could not resist a little sigh of pleasure—it is so childish and honest. You would assume it was written in the nineteenth century by a pious Western moralist. This is the look of the "new humanity" born from the revolution, unless you content yourself with slogans as bombastic as they are hollow.

We move, then, from a concealed Christianity to a socialism into which this Christianity is insinuated. At this point, proponents claim to have found within this socialism a renewed Christianity and the possibility of wedding the two. Likewise, everything is reduced to a historical political praxis, and the discovery of the truth about Jesus is based on this practice. Thus those who believe in "heaven" and those who do not find their common denominator in praxis. The expression "believe in heaven" turns out to be convenient for those who do not believe in it, since such belief means nothing to them. Casalis's use of the term[13] implies that such belief means nothing to him either.

When this praxis is further equated with the force behind history, one can indeed claim that *"every meal taken while sharing historical responsibilities and fellowship has . . . eucharistic value; it is a celebration of struggle and hope, in which Christians and non-Christians together do the truth and can be regarded as disciples united in messianic practice"* (p. 168). Such a statement dismisses Jesus' *"I* am the Truth," with a "No, those who practice politics *do* the truth." This statement also eliminates faith in its transcendent dimension. As long as one is committed to the socialist political struggle, he is a disciple. This incredibly hackneyed statement has been repeated a thousand times by tolerant socialists, but it renders the globalism of the biblical message meaningless.

These same presuppositions, however, also enable Casalis to assert *Vox populi, vox Dei:* the voice of the people is the voice of God. How often have we heard this one! And how can anyone help seeing that this slogan was used by the Catholic Church in the fifth century, as it politicized, trying to found a society on the basis of agreement, synthesis, and a practical syncretism between Christians and pagans (in their ignorant condemnation, many forget that this was the Church's intention in the fourth century, and even much later, before it tried to "convert" using all possible means).

Vox populi, vox Dei. But how can this be? Does it mean that those who make history by their practice accomplish the will of God, whether or not they recognize the God of Jesus Christ? They accomplish exactly what God wills in history? This was indeed the basis from which the Church started. Next the

---

13. As in the French title of his book.—TRANS.

Church used a second saying: *gesta dei per Francos;* that is, the Franks (after all, why not?) bring about the history God wills.

After the Franks, however, just as clearly, the crusaders do the same thing: "God wills it." At this point I realize someone will stop me, saying "The Christians' contention that they make history is unacceptable." But I fail to understand why non-Christians should be the ones to accomplish history as God wills, whereas Christian throngs and even "Christian" states would be unable to do it.

At this point we move on with no hesitation to *Gott mit uns,* God on our side. What God is involved? No matter! God is always with whoever associates Him with a cause! God has been mobilized to serve the cause of class struggle on behalf of the poor and the oppressed, having previously been called on (as He still is!) to serve on the side of the oppressors and propertied people. But this is merely a phase in the traditional use of God in all conflicts. Each side makes use of Him, of course.

As soon as truth is reduced to politics, and the cause of a party is labeled "God's cause," one cannot get off so easily. God and Truth are lost. The *political* "cause" of the poor is no better than any other. The result is always the same, because, as soon as the poor become the most powerful nation in the world, there are no more poor: they become lost and forgotten. Politics is the best possible means for the definitive corruption of poverty.

It is true that the cause of the poor is holy, whereas other causes are not, because (but this "because" is suspect, say Marxist Christians!) Jesus became poor, was the Poor One. But be careful! We have embarked on a fine discussion of praxis (I repeat that this means Marxism), but who says the cause of the poor can be identified with Marxism? Furthermore, as far as the *vox populi* is concerned, Marx never tolerated the idea of the "people" so dear to Proudhon. Marx's proletariat was not composed of all the poor, we must remember (Marx never admitted poor peasants or the non-industrial poor to the proletariat). For that matter, the *populus* of the saying are not just the workers but the *totality of the people,* including nobles, patricians, the rich, etc. Let me say again that only on the basis of rank error can one attempt to find a connection between the intervention of the non-

Christian poor in history and the work of God (or Jesus Christ?), and thus between Marxist theory and authentic Christianity.

Everything we have just analyzed depends on the same tactic: subtle changes in the meanings of words and intellectual confusion enable one to construct a Marxist-Christian edifice, bit by bit. One of the irritating aspects of Casalis's book is its lack of precision and rigorous argument. If I had it in for him, I could say this lack is no accident, since Casalis manages to transport us to the paradise of "correct ideas" precisely by means of this hazy lack of clarity! For example, he talks constantly of "classes," but he never indicates precisely what he means by the term, any more than many other authors do. Does he mean simply the rough, elementary observation that rich and poor, powerful and weak, exist? This distinction holds true in every society.

Marx's term "social class," however, means something entirely different. Marx concretely specifies that the "poor" or the "people" do not constitute a class. Still less are they necessarily oppressed. When Marx widened his concept of class, he hesitated to admit that slaves had constituted a class! Anyone who remains on Casalis's level has no right to speak of classes and class struggle *as if he spoke from a Marxist perspective.* Nor should he speak of taking up the cause of the weak and oppressed as if this constituted the class struggle, when Marx says the opposite. Such shifts in the meaning of terms are fundamental, since they make all people of good will fall into the Communist fly-trap.

As for declaring that class struggle is a scientific theory, a law that determines the history of societies, one would have to ignore history and adhere blindly to an ideology to be able to say so. Absolutely no "scientific theory" or explanation is involved when one observes that conflicts between oppressors and oppressed have always existed!

Another shift in the use of terms: the famous praxis we have already spoken so much about. Casalis carefully avoids defining what Marx understands by praxis; we have seen how complicated the subject is. But Casalis needed to leave the term hazy in order to assimilate it to Christianity: obviously Christianity presupposes a practice, the practice of faith. This practice cannot be merely a private practice of individual values; it amounts necessarily to a practice in society, thus a political practice. But a political practice is a praxis. When we say praxis we are talking about Marx, and where Marx is involved, praxis means class struggle. Therefore, the practice of faith is class struggle, concludes Casalis. Naturally, he is too clever to bring such a coarse sequence out into the open. But the above equivalents in reality dictate the argument of his book, and constitute a trap for the person of good faith who wants to put his faith into practice. He finds himself committed in the end to class struggle (since his practice, if it is not the Communist practice in favor of the poor, inevitably amounts to the capitalist practice of the exploiters and ruling class).

This issue becomes still more difficult, however. Responding to Dumas's question, "Who will decide which practice is correct?," Geoltrain (*Réforme*, April 1978) declares that the answer is clear: Jesus, in concrete acts, opposes the established social, political, and religious structures. He takes the side of the excluded. This practice expresses a choice that is normative, for a Christian. Thus imitating Jesus becomes the criterion of correct practice.

This response, although it is quite traditional in content and renewed in form (since imitating Jesus deals with completely different matters, depending on time and culture), is utterly incorrect from a materialist point of view. Precise Marxist-materialist thought provides a perfectly clear criterion for correct practice: historical efficacy. Nothing else will do. Thus there are two possibilities: either one must attempt to put forward a materialist theology, which could only be Marxist, in which case one is obliged to observe a certain minimum of consistency (retaining Marxism's decisive criterion); or else one must decide that the criterion is imitating Jesus, who was on the side of the poor, the excluded, etc. But in this case, one does not have a criterion for correct *practice* (since this practice is not the choice of a situation but a committed *action* that may lead *anywhere*). Likewise, it is completely useless to burden oneself, in this case, with a lot of pseudo-Marxist mumbo jumbo about class struggle, ruling powers, imperialism, economic exploitation, etc., which forms a kind of ideological haze around Christian commitment. Otherwise, when one chooses to use these terms and speak of class struggle, one must be honest enough to go all the way: the only criterion of correct praxis is historical efficacy!

Casalis indulges in the same looseness and clever shifts in meaning when he speaks of revolution and the poor. Here we have a twofold problem: First, *who* are the poor? Second, what should be done? When we are dealing with a poverty-stricken person who is dying of hunger, the case is clear. But is it enough to give him something to eat?

This twofold question is quite difficult. Who are the poor? Those imprisoned by Communist regimes are poor: in Cambodia, Vietnam, Tibet, etc. So are African victims of their own political regimes, of both the Right and the Left. But a person rich in economic terms and ill or in mourning is also poor, as is the victim of social contempt or hatred. In France today many military and police officers are poor because they belong to professions presently despised.

It is not adequate to lump all the poor together and speak of them generally. When a revolution takes place, the former rich become the poor: the aristocrats in 1793, the wealthy Russian peasant farmers in 1919, the collaborators in France in 1944— these are the poor. But Casalis fails to take them into account. For him only the economically poor count, as a group (a "class," according to Casalis), and only if they are victims of an imperialistic capitalist regime. The rest fail to interest him. I can say unambiguously that the poor for Casalis are *those who are designated as such by socialist doctrine.* This view indicates the extent of ideology's sway over him.

Casalis justifies his stance, of course, asserting that Jesus approached the economically poor. Here again, however, he should realize that such an assertion is historically inaccurate. I refer to our earlier study of publicans and prostitutes, who were poor because despised, rejected, and excluded (as were French black-market profiteers in 1944-45). The centurion was poor because his son was ill. Conversely, the Pharisees, whom Jesus contended with so much, were neither rich in terms of money (they tended to live on a rather poor level), nor an exploiting class! But from Casalis's point of view, one must use the good criteria furnished by Marxist theory—the facts need only sort themselves out accordingly!

As for action in favor of the poor, this, too, is simple. In any case, individual action, springing from personal love, is condemned as hypocrisy designed to rationalize one's class situation. Helping lift an individual poor person from his destitution does not matter so much as politicizing him. In this way one gets at the causes (which can only be capitalism and class exploitation), so that one can raise his consciousness level and involve him in the revolutionary process. This process constitutes the answer to poverty.

The same sorts of shifts in meaning and the same haziness occur in connection with revolution. We hear everywhere that Christians must be revolutionary. I wrote it myself around 1945, and even earlier. But Casalis never touches on the question: What revolution is involved? Clearly he means neither E. Mounier's "necessary revolution" (1937) nor what I called by the same name in 1968. No, for Casalis, there is no point in considering this question; only one revolution exists: the Marxist-Leninist revolution, which leads to Communism, through the suppression of the ruling class.

Since many Christians could agree with the importance of a fundamental revolution, all the while rejecting this particular revolution, it is important to establish what revolution is called for. At the same time, Casalis's suggestions are extremely dangerous, when he speaks with enthusiasm of being militant, of commitment at any price (without specifying *what* commitment and where). Any totalitarian group could approve such assertions.

We could make the same criticism of Casalis's statement that one has the right to speak about action only when one participates in it, from within, in complete sympathy with its objectives. But I have heard such talk a thousand times, from fascists as well as Stalinists: "You have no right to judge from the outside; first you must join up, sympathize totally with our aims, and then you can talk." But that is just when one can no longer say anything! The experience of those who looked horrified, in hindsight, on Hitler's or Stalin's time confirms this: "How could we have taken part in that?" they ask.

Casalis proposes, then, a single revolution, the Communist version; but what does it try to accomplish? Here again we find nothing but nebulous language: he passes over the results of the Communist revolutions. He provides two somewhat specific indications, however. (1) When they take power, the oppressed are infinitely less harsh and cruel than the bourgeois and imperialists were toward them. The reader is of course dumbfounded at this point. When we think of the appalling massacres marking all Communist revolutions since 1917, even in China, we realize that they go far beyond colonialism's worst excesses in Africa. Casalis prefers to ignore this fact, however, refusing to listen to such ideas, just as he refused to listen to talk of concentration camps in the Soviet Union in 1950. On the basis of a doctrinal a priori, the oppressed are necessarily better when they exercise power than were their old oppressors.

(2) In any case, according to Casalis, in Vietnam, Cuba, and Angola, we see the birth of a new, fraternal, human civilization, in which everyone is respected and people can at last aspire to true development. Curiously, Casalis no longer dares give the example of the Soviet Union or China. He refers to small countries where endless poverty is supposed to be overcome. Here again, what illusions and imagination! Why doesn't Casalis mention that revolution *also* plunges people into poverty, and much deeper poverty than previously? The Khmer people have never in the course of their history been reduced to such economic destitution as they have known since 1975. And there are so many other *real* examples like this, to oppose to Casalis's dreams! As for the poverty in Vietnam, I regret to say it has been overcome through the North's exploitation of the South (which was not poverty-stricken).

Do these societies emerging from revolution have the qualities Casalis ascribes to them? It would be better not to insist on Angola, considering its massacres of ethnic groups hostile to the revolution. The majority of the people opposed the Communist movement, so that without Cuba's military aid, the Communist dictatorship could never have been established. Can one speak of a renewed Cuban people? They seem mainly to be an essentially militarized people: their interventions in Angola, Ethiopia (Somalia), and Zaire, involving a total contingent of at least three divisions, are indications of militarism and imperialism. It is true that Cuba is at the Soviet Union's beck and call, like a good little Soviet soldier. I fail to understand, however, why Casalis deplores the Soviet intervention in Czechoslovakia, all the while forgetting about Cuba's interventions!

As for Vietnam the virtuous, such a notion shows the author has learned nothing from the world's successive illusions concerning Communist countries. Clearly the North Vietnamese have had enough, and try to flee however they can; the South Vietnamese sometimes even prefer Cambodia! These are not abominable bourgeois exploiters who are fleeing: they are peasants and mountain people, etc.

Does it make any sense, then, to construct an ideology of revolution and undertake a Marxist rereading of the gospel, only to arrive at such results? We must understand that Communism is *nothing but* a praxis. There is no ideal model of Communism, whose application might sometimes be unfortunate; such thinking shows that one is still a bourgeois idealist. All that exists is a revolutionary praxis; therefore I need not evaluate Communism on the basis of values, scientific qualities, or an ideal, but *only* on the basis of practice: revolutionary praxis. When I see the concrete working out of this praxis, as in the Soviet Union (bureaucracy, dictatorship, conformism, work camps, etc.), China, and assorted satellites, I feel duty bound to say that Marxism in effect negates everything human. I need not attempt a reinterpretation of Scripture in the name of this Marxism— and there is no other. I need not try to construct a materialist theology in the name of such a practice.

In conclusion, we must ask what value such an enterprise could have. We have seen how it originates and by what sociological process it can be explained. In this way we have discovered its significance (in human terms). We have discovered where it comes from, how it spreads, and what it means. But in the last analysis, what is its value?

Our criticisms in these last two chapters are not circumstantial and do not depend on two particular books by Belo and Casalis. We have criticized the very foundation of the operation and its various aspects. Obviously, reinterpreting Scripture and constructing a materialist theology hold no interest for Marxists, and do not lead to a better understanding of Marxism. At best, Christians' agreement and support could serve as a complementary tactic, as Lenin says. But no theology is needed for this purpose.

Conversely, this effort in no way advances theology or biblical understanding. Everything that is considered to be gained by a materialist reading has already been known and gained through other readings. This reading produces only unfortunate confusion. As for the theology, it provides no important advance over classical natural theology. It merely gives a modern touch to the temptations that reappear periodically in the political history of the Church, like so many outbreaks of fever. This theology provides nothing to advance the knowledge of revelation and life in Christ.

I will go even further: as far as the poor are concerned, this theology is the worst of all, since it reduces the gospel to all the earthly promises we have heard for two or three thousand years. It offers nothing beyond what socialism has said to the poor, and deprives them of the unique, irreplaceable dimension that the gospel gives to hope. Materialist theology wants to destroy this dimension (because it has served the ruling classes and because it has turned people's gaze from sociopolitical reality, which is the "only reality"!). Yet only this dimension can satisfy our "desire for eternity." Thus the so-called theology of the poor leaves them poorer, more deprived, imprisoned, and alienated than they were before the failure of socialism, during the period of transcendent theology.

C. Supplementary Notes on Casalis's Book

I realize that it is utterly pedantic to point out errors. But in such a serious debate, we cannot tolerate ignorance or faulty interpretations when they serve as arguments. And Casalis's abundant errors are not inconsequential!

I will pass over his very rudimentary references to Marx. He scarcely goes beyond the *Manifesto*, with one inaccurate quotation from *The German Ideology* and another from the *Contribution to the Critique of Hegel's Philosophy of Right* (p. 212, n. 9). We can dismiss these errors; Casalis would not have had to provide quotations if he had had a genuine knowledge of Marx's thought.

Casalis's errors concerning history are not his own, since he finds them in J.-M. Aubert. The reader is stupefied, however, to learn that Jesus' title (Son of God, Savior) was a classical term reserved for the emperor, especially in use between Augustus and Constantine. This early imperial title was thus supposed to be applied later to Christ. In this fashion it is shown that Jesus' title does not come to Him from the Old Testament, but from pagan politics: this title "indicates a political component within the very notion of salvation" (p. 36). But this view involves a whole fabric of errors: the emperors *never* officially bore the title of Savior. Nor do I believe they were ever called "Son of God": Augustus explicitly refused all titles that could connote divine filiation. He reluctantly permitted a return to the title "Savior" *(Soter)* in the Near East, so as not to break with local custom. After Augustus, the emperor was called *Divus,* that is, "having a god-like nature." But the emperors who took the name *Deus* (Domitian and Caligula) have been considered somewhat mad.

The emperor was called *Dominus* in the western sector of the empire, and *Kyrios* (Lord) in the east. But declaring Jesus as the true *Kyrios* did not constitute a political assimilation of Jesus as emperor. Rather, it was a political act directed toward depriving the emperor of his supreme title.

The Seleucid dynasty in the Middle East used the title *Soter* (and very occasionally Son of God), but always as part of a four-part name: *Soter-Euergete-Epiphane-Poliorkete.* To flatter him, some religious orders transferred these Seleucid titles to the emperor, but this never became official. If it were true that Jesus was called "Savior" *because* this was a royal title, I fail to understand why He was not also given the other three, which suited Him just as well!

In reality, imperial majesty was on the contrary enhanced when the empire became Christian; *at that moment* we can speak of a profound mixing of politics with Christian religious matters. But tracing the source of certain titles of Jesus back to political concerns constitutes erroneous analysis. As far as *Savior* is concerned, it is just like *Kyrios:* a polemical act designed to oust a false savior. It amounts to a refusal of political power rather than a projection of it!

Another incredible error from Aubert: "St. Thomas [Aqui-

nas] makes the nine categories [of the angelic hierarchy] correspond to the political functionaries of the Middle Ages, most of
whom bore titles borrowed from Roman law" (p. 37). Amazing!
Medieval functionaries? Someone should write a thesis to
search them out! Nine categories? How well organized they
were in the Middle Ages! And "titles borrowed from Roman
law"! If we want to talk about Roman functionaries, there were
at least fourteen different ranks in the declining western empire;
and in Byzantium we have six different titles and a dozen func-
tions. Nothing of all this, however, carries over into the West of
the Middle Ages! Where does Aubert find these nine categories
of functionaries in the Middle Ages? A minor error, you say? An
academic quarrel? Of course! Utterly unimportant, except that
*Casalis tries to use this error to prove that theology arises from involve-
ment in politics!* This sort of argument, in which false science is
used to shock the conventionally minded, is detestable.

It is amazing to note the degree to which Casalis uses all
sorts of apparently erudite and scientific arguments to bolster
this thesis. He quotes an important Mexican Amerindian poem
of the seventeenth century, for example (pp. 17-18): the author
describes how happy people were before the whites' arrival,
how misfortune came with Christianity, and how Christians be-
haved like tigers. Casalis quotes the poem as an example of
"non-Christian countertheology" (p. 18). Naturally, he under-
scores that "no argument based on the religious domination exercised by the priests and leaders of 'primitive' peoples could
justify the continuance of restoration of a 'Christian' order";
here I agree with him utterly. But Casalis neglects the fact that
this poem is simply a lie, since the situation in Mexico was
worse before white people arrived on the scene. The Aztec dictatorship over all the people they had conquered and reduced
to slavery (the Toltecs, etc.) was abominable. We have to turn
Casalis's argument around: we must not accept this utterly un-
founded pseudo-countertheology based on the dream of a gold-
en age, just because Christians have made mistakes. Otherwise
we fall into the trap of accepting absolutely anything, just as
long as it upholds our theories!

It would be impossible to point out all Casalis's errors. He
quotes a text written by H. Gollwitzer in 1973 that declares un-

important the "constraints put upon a few intellectuals in the Soviet Union" (since obviously the Soviet Union cannot be faulted for anything else; p. 106). To consider a completely different example, Casalis does not hesitate to make a political translation of the word "bandit" *(lestes)*, deciding it means "'member of a fighting band' of zealots" or "guerrilla" (p. 38). He then presents this as a scientific result (whereas he has twisted the Greek text!). Such examples indicate that the author leaves no stone unturned in his search for ways to undergird his hypotheses.

Chapter VII

Anarchism and Christianity*

1. Anarchism and Socialism
as Potential Allies of Christianity

Perhaps it seems odd to attempt a reconciliation of anarchism and Christianity, since the idea that they are utterly irreconcilable enemies is so well established. Doesn't anarchism repeatedly cry "no God and no Master"? And haven't anarchist thinkers made anti-Christianity, anti-religion, and anti-theism one of the main points of their doctrine? One could argue that Marx's atheism, or even his anti-theism, is secondary, since he deals with the matter more in passing than directly. But Proudhon, P. Kropotkin, and Bakunin oppose God in a major sense. It is true that Marx offers us a long analysis of religion, showing how all revolutions must also be directed against religion as an especially alienating form of ideology. But this issue is after all not essential in Marx.

Looking at the question from the opposite angle, we see that Christianity clearly not only respects authority, but presupposes that authorities exist. Everyone believes Christianity to be a doctrine of order. For John Calvin, certainly anything is preferable to anarchy, which he considers the most dreadful fate for a society; the worst tyrant would be clearly better than an absence of civil authority, which makes people each other's enemy. In such a society each person's sin would act against everyone else without limit or restraint. Obviously the idea of a radically sinful humanity eliminates totally the contemplation of an *an-arché*: the absence of authority and command; without these, a person finds no re-

---

* Originally published in nearly identical form as "Anarchie et christianisme," in *Contrepoint*, no. 15 (1974), 157-73. An earlier version of this article was translated by Ruth Gritsch in *Katallagete*, 7, no. 3 (Fall 1980), 14-24.—TRANS.

sistance to the evil within himself, and thus cuts loose, so that anything can happen in this worst of all imaginable situations.

From both sides, then, the reconciliation of anarchism and Christianity seems excluded. This incompatibility is greater than that of socialism (of whatever stripe) and Christianity. Many Christian thinkers have found idealistic, utopian, romantic socialism quite attractive. Even scientific socialism holds an attraction for Christians, since it is also a doctrine of order and organization: it seeks to bring about justice and concerns itself greatly with the poor. Socialism speaks of freedom, but its freedom is well ordered. Socialism may mention an ultimate disappearance of the state, but this is an insignificant doctrine compared with the great egalitarian transformation it seeks, and which suits the perspective of Christian thought so well. It will be much, much later that the state withers away, so Christians do not find the matter too bothersome.

Looking at it from the other direction, we find that socialism readily recognizes many good aspects of Christianity: love of neighbor, the search for justice, service, the importance of a social goal (rather than just an other-worldly concern), etc. And socialists readily accept Christians as companions traveling down the same road: "those who believe in heaven with those who do not." After all, we can do things together, even if our beliefs differ.

From the Christian perspective, the same thing holds true, expressed in the "part of the way" theory: "since we both want a more just, brotherly, and egalitarian society, let's travel together the part of the road that leads to these goals. Our belief in God is no problem, you see: it has no influence on our social project (identical to yours) or on the political means we use to achieve it. We can go our separate ways *afterward*, when we have reached our goal. Once we are living in a just society, we Christians will reaffirm the importance of faith in Jesus Christ." I have only slightly exaggerated this point of view.

Between anarchists and Christians, however, the same cooperation would not be possible. After all, on the one hand, anarchists make the destruction of religion a central element in their revolution. Without it, no revolution is possible. On the other hand, Christians can hardly conceive of a society without a preestablished and rigorously maintained order.

How shall we reconcile Christianity with anarchism, then? The new school of atheistic Christianity simplifies matters, no doubt. If Christians have decided to kill off God, reconciliation is already half accomplished. Anarchists have very little to add; they find the situation quite satisfactory. Jesus as a good prophet, the pacifist defender of the poor, never presented a problem for anarchists—on the contrary.

At the same time, Christians not only abandon the distasteful doctrine of original sin, the radical evil in humanity, but they add to this an entire theology (if we can call it that) designed to show the centrality of humanity. The "God" (He is called "God," but in reality He does not exist) of the Bible has as His only aim the Kingdom of humanity: the realization, fulfillment, and flowering of human potential; through cultural error this has been called the Kingdom of God. At this point both halves of the road have been covered: anarchists can readily accept Christianity, and Christians can easily participate in anarchism. Oddly enough, this joining of forces has not taken place: neither side feels any attraction for the other. These days being socialist or Marxist and Christian is very well accepted, but no one thinks of marrying anarchism and Christianity.[1]

I believe that this disjunction can be explained by another small obstacle that remains, from the anarchist point of view: the Church. Although the Church presents no problem for Christianity's relationship with socialism (institutions always understand each other; Church and Party amount to the same thing), with anarchism it becomes an annulling obstacle. True, Christians are ready to accept this small additional sacrifice, so that a significant contingent is doing everything it can to destroy the Church. They show the Church as a kind of wart on the face of primitive Christianity, as having completely distorted primitive Christianity. But this attempt scarcely suffices to reassure

---

1. A recent exception to this antipathy between anarchism and Christianity is Vernard Eller, *Christian Anarchy: Jesus' Primacy over the Powers* (Grand Rapids: Eerdmans, 1987), heavily influenced by Ellul.—TRANS.

and convince anarchists. A lot of time will have to pass before
this notion becomes commonly accepted.

From the Christians' point of view, there is an even larger obstacle to marriage with anarchism—a political one. All Christians prepared to accept the theological reshuffling we have alluded to are politically to the Left, or to the extreme Left. But
who knows what anarchism is?[2] From the point of view of the
"good" Left of the Marxist, anarchists are double-crossing, un-
scientific dreamers. Moreover, Marx condemned Proudhon and
Bakunin. In view of the fact that freedom remains the anarchists'
central imperative, they belong to the Right (since freedom has
been the Right's rallying cry since 1945).

No doubt anarchism restored its fortunes somewhat in 1968,
but only to fall into radical Leftism. The serious Left, which goes
as far as Trotskyism but no farther, roundly condemned anar-

---

2. Let me indicate here that I have long affirmed the anarchist position as the only acceptable stance in the modern world. This in no way
means that I believe in the possibility of the realization and existence of
an anarchist society. All my position means is that the present center of
conflict is the state, so that we must adopt a radical position with respect
to this unfeeling monster. As early as 1947, I was labeled an "anarchist
Christian" in a list of French Protestants' political options. I bring this
point up because some confusion still remains in this connection. Dumas
criticizes the position of Casalis's book as anarchist. And in his response
to Dumas, Geoltrain claims that Dumas indulges in mere name-calling.
Geoltrain identifies the real issue as the relationship with political power.
These are strange errors, since throughout his book Casalis shows strict
adhesion to Marx's thought and doctrine, and never betrays any anarchist tendencies.

We must remember that Marxism and anarchism are utterly irreconcilable enemies; Bakunin's criticism of Marx is entirely justified, as later
events have shown. If the "real issue" is our relationship with political
power, as Geoltrain says (and I am only partly in agreement here, since
the "real issue" is also our relationship with technique), then that
completely undermines the Marxist-Christians' position. This is true because Marxism gives us a false analysis of the state; Marx's error led inevitably to the Soviet state.

As far as biblical criticism of political power is concerned, I began this
in 1937, and I do not believe that Casalis or Marxist Christians add anything to what we have known for a long time—except for their unfortunate tendency to confuse the issue!

chism at that point. Organization, after all, indicates one is responsible—along with efficiency and consistent tactics, which imply management. Leftist Christians could hardly fail to accept such criteria. But anarchists?

No, chaos can hardly suit Christians. And how can one separate anarchy from chaos? Anarchism remains unrelated to Christianity, then, since both traditional and Leftist Christians reject it. But the other disheartening matter is that nothing remains of Christianity, except for Jesus' name, what with the abandonment of God the Father or God as personal, the reduction of Jesus to a historical human model, the coming of humanity's reign, the expansion of human power, and the suppression of the Church.

In the following pages I would like to outline another way of reconciling anarchism and Christianity. I do not intend to abandon the biblical message in the slightest, since it seems to me, on the contrary, that biblical thought leads straight to anarchism—anarchism is the only "anti-political political position" in harmony with Christian thought.

2. Anarchism's Quarrel with Christianity

First we must try to elucidate the nineteenth-century anarchists' quarrel with Christianity, religion, and the Church (twentieth-century anarchists have taken up this quarrel without renewing or enriching it!). Bakunin gives us the best summary of the matter, in *God and the State:*

> God being everything, the real world and man are nothing. God being truth, justice, goodness, beauty, power, and life, man is falsehood, iniquity, evil, ugliness, impotence, and death. God being master, man is the slave. Incapable of finding justice, truth, and eternal life by his own effort, he can attain them only through a divine revelation. But whoever says revelation says revealers. . . . and these, once recognized as the representatives of divinity on earth . . . necessarily exercise absolute power. All men owe them passive and unlimited obedience; for against the divine reason . . . no terrestrial justice holds. Slaves of God, men must also be slaves of Church and State, *in so far as the State is consecrated by the Church.* This truth Christianity, better than all other religions . . . understood. . . . That is why Christianity is

the absolute religion . . . the Roman Church is the only consistent, legitimate, and divine church.[3]

The idea of God implies the abdication of human reason and justice; it is the most decisive negation of human liberty, and necessarily ends in the enslavement of mankind, both in theory and practice. . . .

If God is, man is a slave; now, man can and must be free; then, God does not exist.

I defy anyone whomsoever to avoid this circle. . . .

This contradiction lies here: they [Christians] wish God, and they wish humanity. They persist in connecting two terms which, once separated, can come together again only to destroy each other. They say in a single breath: "God and the liberty of man," "God and the dignity, justice, equality, fraternity, prosperity of men"—regardless of the fatal logic by virtue of which, if God exists. . . . he is necessarily the eternal, supreme, absolute master, and, if such a master exists, man is a slave; now, if he is a slave, neither justice, nor equality, nor fraternity, nor prosperity are possible for him. In vain, flying in the face of good sense and all the teachings of history, do they represent their God as animated by the tenderest love of human liberty: a master, whoever he may be and however liberal he may desire to show himself, remains none the less always a master. His existence necessarily implies the slavery of all that is beneath him. Therefore, if God existed, only in one way could he serve human liberty—by ceasing to exist.

A jealous lover of human liberty, and deeming it the absolute condition of all that we admire and respect in humanity, I reverse the phrase of Voltaire, and say that, *if God really existed, it would be necessary to abolish him.*[4]

---

3. At this point we see clearly the degree to which Bakunin has been influenced by culture. In reality, the reasoning he reconstructs, going from the general to the particular, amounts to the reverse: the Catholic Church supports the state. Bakunin believes he finds the Church historically to be the most authoritarian and anti-liberal structure that has ever existed (he appeals to history to prove the truth of his statements about God). Thus Christianity (of which Catholicism represents the extreme) is authoritarian and anti-liberal, and so are religions (Christianity being the most perfected one). From here Bakunin moves to religion, and finally to religion's object: he sees God as the authoritarian master and inspiration of all the rest. I have given Bakunin's real argument, but he reverses it in order to render it philosophical and warranted.

4. *God and the State* (Freeport, NY: Books for Libraries Press, repr. 1971), pp. 24-28.

In my opinion Bakunin offers the best résumé of anarchist thought concerning God and human freedom.[5] Naturally, we would have to add two items to this: (1) all Proudhon's writings on authority (all authorities depend on God), on the sovereign wording of laws based on the Decalogue (the general idea of the revolution), and on the Church's role in the denial of free inquiry; (2) the scientistic position adopted by anarchists in the second half of the nineteenth century. They attempted to prove that God does not exist, on the basis of the development of science (see S. Faure and E. Reclus, for example). But these additions seem less important to me than Bakunin's summary, concerning which I have four remarks to make:

(1) What strikes us most in Bakunin's statement against God, religion, and the Church is its circumstantial quality, which dates it. All his reproaches and attacks seem tied to the concrete historical circumstances of Christianity's evolution.

The central theological issue is the very concept of God. Since the thirteenth century, many Christian theologians have insisted on the power of God. God has been conceived, above all, and even exclusively, as All-Powerful, the King, the Autocrat, the radical Judge, the Terrible One. When anarchism vows "no God and no Master," it takes aim at this kind of God. Such a God in effect excludes human freedom: a human being is merely a plaything in His hands. One has no possibility of being, and is damned a priori. We can easily understand why a doctrine asserting human dignity cannot accept such a God.

God is further seen as the Creator: not only the Creator, but the One who determines everything. He allocates good and evil, misfortune and blessing. How strange that the biblical God of Jesus Christ has been so distorted. Jesus, calling on the Father

---

5. Let me make it clear that when I speak here of anarchism, I refer mainly to the great classical anarchists, but also include the active groups of the Jura Federation and anarchist unions. I do not refer to nihilism, a somewhat divergent historical branch of anarchism. Without intending to eliminate the nihilists and violent anarchists, I consider that they pose a complementary problem (as opposed to the central problem) in the relationship between Christianity and anarchism: the problem of violence. Violence is an essential problem concerning means, but not the true crux of the issue, which is *an-arché:* the absence of authority.

as His authority, chooses the way of radical nonviolence. The
God of Jesus chooses to become incarnate in a Baby in order to
reveal Himself.

Love is the only "definition" of God given in the Bible. Beginning with the Exodus, this biblical God acts in liberation: He is
above all the Liberator par excellence. He condemns sin and the
powers of evil because they alienate humanity. Even in the Old
Testament, where God's power is often emphasized, it is *never,
never* presented by itself. Every proclamation of power is associated with (and often surrounded by) a proclamation of love,
pardon, an exhortation to reconciliation, an affirmation that
God's power acts *for* people and never *against* them. The All-
Powerful taken as the image of the biblical God is as mistaken as
the painting showing God as a bearded old man seated above
the clouds. When I say this, I am not doing the same thing as the
theologians of the death of God. They annul 90% of the biblical
text, and then continue to speak incessantly of God, whether in
a cultural context or otherwise. I limit myself to rehabilitating the
concept of God, which classical theology distorted.

(2) I will not elaborate on my second remark concerning
Bakunin's text: his identifying religion with revelation, or religion with Christian faith. This error is beginning to be widely
understood. Marx called religion "the opium of the people," but
the anarchists' much stronger criticism of religion is correct. In
the final analysis, however, this criticism has little or nothing to
do with Christian faith.

(3) Concerning another of Bakunin's points, it is true that
Christianity in the form of a religion (with an All-Powerful God)
has supported the established order. Here again we discover a
major distortion stemming in part from the institutionalization
of the Church (which went from being an assembly of people
united only by love, in the same faith, to being an organization
with power). As the institutionalization of the Church hardens,
so does its dogmatism: truth considered as a possession (in
which case it ceases to be truth) leads to judgment and condemnation. Love when institutionalized produces authority and
hierarchy.

Thus the Church was the joyous outcome of the unity of
believers confident of their salvation, as they met together and

showed forth God's love. But it became a structure, a custodian of authority and truth, representing God's power on earth. "No salvation outside the Church" originally meant that those who recognized that Jesus Christ had saved them met together to give thanks (thus, outside the Church, there were no people living this faith). But the phrase came to mean that all those who are outside the framework of the Church are doomed! This reversal of meaning is quite a serious matter.

(4) Finally, Bakunin rightly charges that the Church has come to support the establishment in the form of political powers and social organization. Everyone knows how the Church has continually changed sides so as to fall into line with the present power and become the stoutest supporter of whatever government happens to be in power. Usually the Church has changed sides only to align itself with a "legitimate" government, but not always. Also well known is the bourgeoisie's monstrous use of Christianity, in order to maintain the social order and keep workers obedient.

All these errors, distortions, heresies (I use the word advisedly), and deviations, which produce anti-Christianity, have always existed as potential interpretations of the biblical revelation. But they were accentuated at the Reformation and became the rule in the eighteenth century. By then the bourgeoisie's transformation of theology, the Church, and the relationship of Church and society had become dominant.

Anarchist attacks on God, the Church, and religion are quite accurate, as long as we clarify that they criticize God as modified by this bourgeois theology, and Church as the power it had become. This incidental association of the Church with political and social power should in no way be construed as the expression of biblical Christianity, since it represents rather the reverse (whose root is always the heresy of God conceived of exclusively as All-Powerful).

The anarchists (and Marx) erred in believing they had come face to face with Christianity itself, whereas they had found only its bourgeois transformation. Following this perspective, certain aspects of primitive and medieval Christianity were magnified in order to confirm this view, instead of being considered as mere possibilities, among others. The death of Ananias and

Sapphira, for example, was emphasized to show the apostles as terrible dictators. The Inquisition became the symbol of the medieval Church, and the building of cathedrals showed the enslavement of the poor populace, crushed by the clergy. All reality of love, joy, and liberation, also lived by Christianity in these periods, is gleefully omitted. In other words, in their just battle against Christian totalitarianism and authoritarianism in the seventeenth to nineteenth centuries, anarchists adopted a false view of the basic reality of Christianity and the God of Jesus Christ. We need, then, to correct this error made by anarchism.

Atheism or the absence of God is by no means a necessary condition for anarchism: the presence of the God of Jesus Christ is the necessary condition for human liberation. Denial of this necessity has caused the failure of all the so-called liberating revolutions. Each of these has led to a worse degree of slavery, since human revolution, left to itself, always results in human slavery unless people are given freedom as their reference point and requirement—a freedom that radically transcends them. Freedom won in a context of humanity as absolute leads inevitably to the establishment of dictatorship.

Arriving at real freedom requires the relativization of all human pretensions and therefore of all human dominations. This relativization takes place only if humanity recognizes an exterior limit that transcends it, and if the transcendent limit is liberating love (as in the Christian revelation). No relativization takes place if humanity tries to limit itself, since this cannot be done if humanity considers itself absolute and proclaims its reign. We will return to this point in our final section.

Thus the deviation of Christianity gave rise to the anarchists' valid criticism, but they failed to understand adequately that they were attacking a deviation rather than the reality (which is on occasion lived out, after all!). Since they failed to appreciate the truth of the revelation, they took exception to a socio-theological idea of God rather than to the God of the Bible and Jesus Christ.

3. Political Power in the Bible

Now we shall consider the other side of the coin, beginning with the biblical data. What does the Old Testament teach concerning political power? On the one hand, it *always* challenges political power in itself where the "nations" are concerned. The Old Testament claims repeatedly that these kings consider themselves gods, but they will be destroyed in order to manifest their weakness.

Even, for example, in the case of Israel's deportation to Babylon, when the prophets instruct the people to work for the good of the *society* in which they live, there is no question of supporting the Babylonian king. One can consider the kings of Assyria and Egypt as instruments chosen to show forth God's anger, but they have no legitimacy. Elijah is sent to anoint the new king of Syria, but this means only that this king will become God's scourge to chastise Israel. Elijah enters no alliance, gives no support to this king.[6] The government of a foreign people never appears in the Old Testament as legitimate or satisfactory.[7] At best such a government is seen as a necessity: no alternative is available. The relationship with these political powers involves only conflict; one can expect nothing but persecution, war, devastation, famine, and evil from these kings.

Only two representatives of Israel collaborate with a foreign king: Joseph and Daniel. But we must remember that Joseph, who brings his brothers to Egypt through his success, produces nothing but the slavery of all Israel! Such cooperation as a *fact* matters little, since here we are examining how Israel *looks at* political power. Israel's attitude is revealed more by its myths than by "historical" accounts. The most one can expect, then, is a "favor" or a *temporary* alliance, which then leads inevitably to slavery, domination, and oppression.

Daniel provides our second example (likewise, the problems of his historical existence and the fictional nature of the narrative matter little; on the contrary, he becomes more representative if invented!). As a great diviner and interpreter of

6. See my *The Politics of God and the Politics of Man*, trans. and ed. Geoffrey W. Bromiley (Grand Rapids: Eerdmans, 1972).

7. Cyrus, the only exception to this, represents a special case.

dreams,[8] Daniel has found favor with Nebuchadnezzar, but this favor has its risks: when Daniel refuses to submit to the king concerning his faith, he is thrown into the fiery furnace (power *must* be worshiped!). Darius throws him into the lions' den. Power is dangerous and devouring; participating in political action and reflection on behalf of the government is an undertaking that inevitably puts true faith in danger. Such participation can lead only to proclaiming the end of this power and to its destruction. We must remember that Daniel remains a prophet of doom for the different kings he serves. He announces to each one the end of his reign, the destruction of the kingdom, the death of the king, etc. Consequently, he negates power to its face, in a sense, even if he serves it temporarily.

You could say that all the above can be explained by the fact that the "nations," Israel's enemies, are involved: pagan and idolatrous peoples God has not chosen, so that Israel's utterly negative judgment of their political power arises from hostility. We must look at royalty in Israel in order to clarify this point. I have written several times on the meaning of this royalty.[9] Rather than repeating my arguments here, I will limit myself to indicating their general outline and my conclusions.

---

8. Further, we must note that both Joseph and Daniel are sought out by government power for very ambiguous reasons: they are the king's diviners. Kings consider them as related to a mysterious power rather than to the truth. They can enlighten the ruler through magic and sorcery. In other words, we have here the seizing of God's gift and its transformation into its opposite. Political power cannot recognize the true God for what He is. It can only use Him, incidentally, for its own reinforcement. This situation offers us a remarkable view of the alliance of the Church with the power structure!

9. I study the implantation of kingship in Israel in "Le Droit biblique d'après l'exemple de la royauté et les cultures orientales," in *Mélanges offerts à Jean Brethe de la Gressaye* (Bordeaux: Editions Bière, 1967), pp. 253-73. I am of course aware of the hypothesis that there were two tendencies: one pro-monarchist, and the other anti-monarchist, so that the apparently contradictory texts have an explanation. Both tendencies clearly existed, but this hypothesis fails to explain the main meaning of the texts (which I cannot discuss here in detail). In particular, the hypothesis does not explain how the anti-monarchist texts were collected and preserved during the monarchic period, and then included with revealed Scripture!

The main text is clearly 1 Samuel 8, the institution of kingship. Up to this point the people of Israel have been without political organization, led "directly by God." When necessary, God sent a "judge" as a temporary, charismatic, provisional leader. But Israel wanted organization—political power, a king—for the sake of efficiency, and to *resemble other peoples*, all of which had kings. Samuel struggles at length to prevent Israel's betrayal of God. God finally yields to His people's disobedience, declaring that "they have rejected me from being king over them" (1 Sam. 8:7).

This very detailed, complex passage boils down to three observations: (1) political power rests on distrust and rejection of God; (2) political power is always dictatorial, excessive, and unjust (1 Sam. 8:10-18); (3) political power is established in Israel through conformity, in imitation of what is done everywhere else.

Israel's first king, Saul, is a raving madman. Then, by grace and as an exception, God chooses David, making him His representative. But David is just a ray of light, showing that God can bring miraculous good from human evil. Solomon shows how exceptional David was; though admirably well equipped for the exercise of power, Solomon ends up radically corrupted by power. His accumulation of wealth and women, his setting up of an independent political power, his establishment of cities, etc.— these can all be considered normal actions for a political power. But these activities produce Solomon's estrangement from God, and finally his rejection. The Bible indicates clearly that Solomon's exercise of political power corrupted a man who began as wise, good, and humble.

Two additional observations: (1) The books of Chronicles, as they describe the kings following Solomon in Israel and Judah, offer us a very strange assessment of political power. Systematically (I insist on this concept as essential for understanding the appraisal of power here; the significance of the word "systematically" only increases if the accounts in Chronicles are not factual!), *all* those shown objectively to be "great" kings historically are represented as bad kings: idolatrous, unjust, tyrannical, murderous. These kings brought about better political organization, made conquests, and enriched their people. In other words, they exercised power "normally." (2) On the contrary, when it comes to historically weak kings, those who lost their wars, allowed their administration to unravel, and lost wealth, Chronicles considers these as good kings. This observation could mean that the only acceptable power in the long run is the weakest one. Or it could mean that if a political leader is faithful to God, he is necessarily a poor political leader, and vice versa. The utter consistency on this issue in Chronicles shows its significance. As far as I know, no other chronicle or historiography, in any country in the world, uses this approach; everywhere else, one considers the successful king as great and legitimate.

One final matter with respect to the Old Testament: a thorough analysis (I skip over details in this brief synthesis) of the coronation procedure and the names used to designate kings shows that the king is never considered to have value in himself. The king is never anything but the current, temporary, incidental sign of the One who is to come. The Coming One defines the present king, who has no importance. He serves merely as a signpost, a pointer that anticipates. God accepts political power to the degree that it points ahead to the ultimate perfection of the Messiah and the Kingdom.

Political power never has any value in itself. On the contrary, Scripture radically repudiates, challenges, and condemns it whenever it claims to exist as political power rather than as a sign. Political power's only value depends on something coming in the future (uncertain at best!) and on what it signifies (the unknown!). We can therefore conclude that the Old Testament never in any way validates any political power. On the contrary, the Scriptures consistently challenge it.

Moving now to the New Testament, we seem to find, as everyone knows, two tendencies: (1) the first, favorable with respect to power (seen mainly in Paul's famous "there is no authority except from God," Rom. 13:1); (2) the other, much more extensive, hostile to power (seen in the Gospels and Revelation).[10] Strangely, the official Church since Constantine has

---

10. In this connection see, among others, O. Cullmann, *The State in the New Testament* (New York: Charles Scribner's Sons, 1956), and my "Rap-

consistently based almost its entire "theology of the State" on Romans 13 and the parallel texts in Peter's epistles.

If we consider Jesus' attitude toward power in the Gospels, we can say without hesitation that He had a radically negative stance. He refused to exercise a judicial type of power, and recommended that His disciples not act like the kings of the nations ("You know that those who are supposed to rule over the Gentiles lord it over them, and their great men exercise authority over them. But it shall not be so among you," Mark 10:42-43). He refused to be king and enter the political conflicts of His time. In this connection it is very significant that Jesus had among His disciples both "collaborators" of the Romans (Matthew) and Zealots (Judas, Simon), violent anti-Roman patriots. He was perfectly acquainted with the resistance party, but refused to join it.

Jesus held power up to ridicule (the famous incident in Matt. 17:24-27, in which a shekel found in a fish's mouth served to pay the tax:[11] the only miracle of this extravagant type, precisely to show that the obligation to pay the tax is ridiculous!). He submitted to Herod's governmental jurisdiction without giving any sign that He recognized its validity; it was the jurisdiction of power, but no more.

We must clarify two sayings of Jesus: (1) The famous "Render to Caesar" (Matt. 22:21). In no way does Jesus favor here the division of the exercise of power into two realms. Exegetes have arrived at unbelievable conclusions based on this passage: God's realm as heaven, spiritual matters, and feelings, with Caesar perfectly entitled to exercise his power over the people and things of this world. Jesus' saying means nothing like this interpretation. He said these words in connection with a second conversation about tax payment, and concerning a coin. The image on the coin is Caesar's; it marks the coin as his property. Give him this money, then (Jesus by no means legitimizes the tax!). Jesus means that Caesar, as *creator* of this money, is its

---

pels et réflexions sur une théologie de l'état," in Jacques Jullien, Pierre l'Huillier, and Jacques Ellul, *Les Chrétiens et l'état*, Eglises en Dialogue, no. 3 (Tours: Maison Mame, 1967), pp. 127-80.

11. As the text indicates, the temple tax is at issue here; but, beginning with the Roman conquest, it had become a public tax.

master—nothing more (we must not forget that for Jesus money belongs to the realm of mammon, a satanic realm!).

As for "the things that are God's" (Matt. 22:21), how could a pious Jew of Jesus' time take this expression as meaning anything but "everything"? As Creator, God is the master of life and death. Everything depends on Him. Jesus' words mean that Caesar is the legitimate master of nothing, except for what he makes himself (and it belongs to the order of the demonic!).

(2) "My kingship is not of this world" (John 18:36). This saying states explicitly that Jesus does not choose to exercise political power. It in no way suggests that Jesus recognizes the validity of such power—on the contrary. Apart from the Kingdom of God, any power exercised is evil, should be obliterated, denied, etc. So Jesus does not represent an apolitical or spiritual attitude; rather, he launches a fundamental attack on power. Rather than showing indifference to what politics can be or do, Jesus expresses His refusal of politics in this passage. No gentle dreamer who looks down from the sky, Jesus challenges the validity of the earthly kingdom. He refuses its power because it does not conform to God's will. This is still true, whether power is exercised by the proletariat, Communists, etc. Power does not change its spiritual nature when it changes hands.

The temptation narrative confirms Jesus' attitude toward political power: in the third temptation in Matthew the devil shows Jesus all the kingdoms of the world and says to Him, "All these I will give you, if you will fall down and worship me" (Matt. 4:9). Jesus responds by refusing to worship him.[12] But He does not dispute Satan's claim by saying that these kingdoms and their political power do not belong to him. On the contrary, Jesus implicitly agrees: Satan can give political power. But a person can exercise political power only if he worships the power of evil.

---

12. I disagree totally with the many exegetes (including R. de Pury) who try to reduce this text to the problem of worship, saying that what Jesus refuses is not political power but the worship of Satan. The text is clear, however: Jesus does not break the connection between power and worship. He agrees implicitly that if He were to worship Satan, he would give Him all this world's kingdoms. Consequently, Jesus does not challenge the satanic nature of power!

This consistent teaching of the Gospels finds its most violent expression in the book of Revelation.[13] Here political power (temporarily represented by Rome, but Revelation sees beyond Rome) takes the form of a beast: one that rises from the sea and symbolizes the state perfectly, in minute detail. A second beast rises from the earth, symbolizing political propaganda. Furthermore, political power is represented at the beginning of Revelation by the red horseman with the sword (whose only function is making war, exercising power, and causing human beings to perish), and at the end by Babylon, the focus of political power, the power of money, and the structure of the city.

Thus we find ourselves in the presence of a consistent biblical series of negations of political power, of witnesses to its lack of validity and legitimacy.[14] Opposite these, we have the Romans 13 text and its parallels. Among these parallels, however, we must make a distinction between the passages that mention only praying for the authorities (a service we render them, perhaps related to the problem of the *exousiai;* we pray so that the authorities will not fall into the hands of demons) and the texts requiring obedience and submission. Romans 13 stands as the only text appearing to provide a general basis for submission.

I believe that it is important to place these *few* texts within the context we have indicated: what common political attitude do we find among Christians of the first generation? A rejection of the authorities (and not only a refusal to worship Caesar).

---

13. For details, see my *Apocalypse: The Book of Revelation*, trans. George W. Schreiner (New York: Seabury, 1977).

14. We must emphasize that the teaching given by this series of biblical texts is not circumstantial. The early Christians did not express their anarchism, their anti-political stance, because of persecutions or the political power's opposition to believers. Theirs is a fundamental attitude. From the beginning, they base everything on the fact that two political authorities conspired to crucify Jesus: the radical nature of their opposition could hardly be better expressed! If anyone contends that these stances are merely circumstantial, then *everything* in the Gospels and the life of Jesus must be considered in the same light. Jesus' teaching in the parables of the Kingdom, or concerning the law, for example, would all be strictly circumstantial.

This refusal leads very quickly to a refusal, for example, to do military service.[15] Consequently, Paul's text appears to be a re-action against the extremism of the anti-political, anarchist posi-tion. Basically, he says: "Don't go too far; don't go to extremes in your refusal. After all, authority comes from God, who has *re-duced* the magistrate to the level of servant (whereas he claims to be the master). The good in society certainly falls far short of the Word of God, but this good amounts to something, after all—and the magistrate guarantees it."

Furthermore, we must combine with this interpretation another matter, brought to light by F. J. Leenhardt: we must not separate Paul's famous saying on the authorities from its con-text. Romans 12 speaks to us of love, and suggests several ap-plications of it. Paul ends his chapter with love of enemies ("if your enemy is hungry, feed him," v. 20, for example). Further-more, immediately following Romans 13:1-7 on the authorities, Paul returns to the theme of love, showing how it sums up all the commandments (vv. 8-10). Then he digresses briefly, deal-ing with the end of history (vv. 11-13), only to return to love, as shown in tolerance toward the weak (v. 14).

Obviously, the verses on the authorities are included within Paul's teaching on love. I would go so far as to summarize them in this fashion: "Love your enemies. No doubt we all consider the authorities our enemies; we must love them, too, however." But since Paul gives a specific reason for loving in each case he considers (the Church, the brethren, enemies, the law, the weak in faith, etc.), he does the same for the authorities. It is in this connection that he writes his famous "there is no authority ex-cept from God" (Rom. 13:1; we must emphasize the negative construction here, as opposed to its later formulation, suggest-ing a principle: *omni potestas a Deo*, all power comes from God). This text, it seems to me, should be reduced to its real meaning: rather than giving us the last word on the matter of political authority, it seeks to apply love in a context where Christians detested the authorities.

---

15. J.-M. Hornus has demonstrated this very well, in *Evangile et La-barum* (Geneva: Labor et Fides, 1960).

4. Christians as Anarchists

Essentially, then, both the Old and New Testaments take exception to all political power. No power can claim to be legitimate in itself. Political power and organization are necessities in society, but only necessities. They attempt repeatedly to take God's place, since magistrates and kings invariably consider themselves the incarnation of authority. We must continually challenge, deny, and object to this power. It becomes acceptable only when it remains on a humble level, when it is weak, serves the good (how rarely does this happen!), and genuinely transforms itself into a servant (of people, since it already serves God!).

Usually, however, this principle is stated the other way: the state is legitimate except when it becomes tyrannical, unjust, violent, etc. In reality, since the state is illegitimate, it should be destroyed, except when it acts as servant of all (in reality, not just rhetorically!), effectively protecting the good. Here I cannot go into how, historically, the Church has completely reversed biblical teaching on this point. We can emphasize, though, that this tendency has persisted.

Without a doubt the official Church, transformed into a power, taught the opposite of biblical teaching. But throughout church history movements arose that we should call anarchist (we discover more about these movements all the time). They deserve this name because, from the Anchorites to N. Berdyaev and L. Tolstoi, they have reaffirmed in different ways the impossibility of the state. No doubt these movements (most of them "spiritual") appear slightly mad—the established Church, especially, has looked at them this way—but they all gave witness to a profound truth of Christianity (sometimes by means of heresies that became more extreme in order to oppose the Church!). These were anarchist movements rather than mere incidental protests against a given power or abuse. They represented rather the very teaching of the Word of God.

Berdyaev, it seems to me, was the last to show the radical incompatibility of the gospel and the state.[16] He demonstrated the

---

16. Nicolas Berdyaev, *Slavery and Freedom,* trans. R. M. French (New York: Charles Scribner's Sons, 1944; French ed. 1938); idem, *The Realm of*

opposition between the ethics of the gospel and the ethics of power (which proclaims as moral what is otherwise forbidden, when its interest is at stake), and between service (central to the application of Christianity) and power. He emphasized that power gives rise to corruption. He would readily accept the well-known concept that "power corrupts; absolute power corrupts absolutely."

Berdyaev contends that the state's well-being and prosperity do not represent the well-being and prosperity of the governed, and still less of all people. The equation of the state's well-being with that of its people is an abominable lie. The state's prosperity always implies the death of innocents. Faith in the state means that to save the state, we must go so far as to sacrifice the innocent. "The death of one man, of even the most insignificant of men, is of greater importance and is more tragic than the death of states and empires. It is to be doubted whether God notices the death of the great kingdoms of the world; but He takes very great notice of the death of an individual man."[17]

Church and state relations represent one form of the relationships between the Spirit and Caesar; Jesus Christ puts our back to the wall, obliging us to choose between them rather than trying to reconcile them! The Church has continually played false in this relationship: by becoming the state's partner, it has become an anti-Church. Christianity's historical sin has been to recognize the state. This sin continues, no matter what form the state takes, no matter who holds power. Recognition of the divine right of kings becomes recognition of the divine right of the people, and later the right of the proletariat: in all cases the sovereignty and the sacred character of power persist!

"What we must refuse, is the sovereignty of the state," says Berdyaev.[18] I have often written that there is no given Christian form of power. This is because, in reality, the only Christian political position consistent with revelation is the negation of power: the radical, total refusal of its existence, a fundamental

---

Spirit and the Realm of Caesar, trans. Donald A. Lowrie (New York: Harper & Brothers, 1952; repr. Westport, CT: Greenwood, 1975; French ed. 1946).

17. Berdyaev, *Slavery and Freedom*, p. 144.

18. *The Realm of Spirit and the Realm of Caesar*, p. 72.

questioning of it, no matter what form it may take. I repeat this statement not so Christians will turn toward some sort of spiritualism, political ignorance, or apolitical position—certainly not! On the contrary, as Christians we must participate in the political world and the world of action, but in order to deny them, to oppose them by our conscious, well-founded refusal. Only this refusal can challenge and occasionally impede the unlimited growth of power. Thus Christians can take their place only beside anarchists; they can never join the Marxists, for whom the state is unacceptable only to the extent that it is bourgeois.

Do Christians contribute anything specific or special to anarchism? Have they a particular service to offer, or are they merely more numbers for the rank and file? I believe Christians have an important role to play in this area, on two different levels. (1) Anarchists live in an illusion, believing that it is possible actually to abolish power and all its sources. They become militant in order to conquer and prevail. Christians must be more realistic. We live in a world that has always been subject to power. I realize that this is no argument: we could begin a new epoch; we must not believe that what has always been will always be. Right. But this attitude would represent a leap into the unknown.

Today we can no longer believe in one of the absolute tenets of anarchist faith: the inevitability of progress. The change from an inferior form of society to a superior form will not necessarily take place. Anarchism and a society of freedom have been promised by no one. More than likely, they will never come into being. If we say this, the anarchist stops in his tracks, discouraged, and asks: "Why bother, then?" Here is where the Christian comes in. Every human action, compared with God's grace, is strictly relative. Human action must be carried out, however, not for the sake of its absolute success (which can take place only in the Kingdom of God), but because we express love in this relative context. Jesus gives us this promise: "You have been faithful over a little, I will set you over much" (Matt. 25:21, 23). We must also understand, however, that human love, such as that of a woman and a man, does not reside in some spectacular declaration, brilliant action, or erotic paroxysm, but in a thousand humble signs of attentiveness which express that the other person counts in a fundamental way more than I do.

We must not become discouraged, then, if our anarchist declaration fails to lead to an anarchist society, or if it does not overthrow society, destroying its whole framework. In any case, this destruction would amount to another manifestation of power, which could only lead, inevitably, to a reconstitution of power. What does this statement mean, then? Just this: that political power, in its essence, tends to grow without limit. It has no reason to limit itself. No constitution or ethic can prevent power from becoming totalitarian. It must discover outside itself, over against it, a radical negation, leading to the establishment of an opposition group that will not aim to conquer power (and thus act politically) or to exercise power for the good of others (and thus be political).

Political power must be encountered by a group that represents both an uncompromising moral conscience and an effective opposing force—a group that is not a class, not organized in advance as a sociological reality. This group's permanent struggle seeks freedom for others. Freedom can be obtained only when we strive for it; no power can give freedom to people. Challenging power is the only way to make freedom a reality. Freedom exists if the negation of political power is strong enough, and when people refuse to be taken in by the idea that freedom will surely come tomorrow, if only. . . . No, there is no tomorrow. Freedom exists today or not at all. When we shake the edifice, we produce a crack, a gap in the structure, in which a human being can briefly find his freedom, which is always threatened.

In order to bring this bit of play into the system, however, we must bring to it a radical, total refusal. Any concession to power enables the totality of power to rush into the small space we have opened. Thus only an anarchist position can conceivably maintain this play within the system that permits freedom. We must not, however, delude ourselves with the vain hope that we will completely destroy this power and then build an ideal society of brotherhood . . . the day after tomorrow. I can hear the disillusioned anarchist: "Is that all we are doing?" Yes: *all* that; through our refusal, we keep the trap from closing all the way, for today. We can still breathe out in the open. The Christian must enable the anarchist to make the transition from a contemptuous "Is that all?" to an "All that," filled with hope.

(2) Christians play another role alongside anarchists. In most cases, anarchists believe that human beings are good by nature, having been corrupted by society or, even better, by power. The state is at fault if criminals exist. Apparently one must believe in this original human goodness in order to hope for the establishment of an anarchist society. In such a society individuals would have to do spontaneously what is best for all, without trying to infringe on their neighbors' domain or freedom. They would have to control their passions and anger, choose to work freely for the community, refrain from troubling order, etc. Otherwise, anarchy would amount to what its opponents accuse it of being: mere disorder, a ghastly war of individuals. To my knowledge, only Bakunin has had the courage to propound the hypothesis that human beings are evil. On it he bases important conclusions for his plan to organize society.

We need to go further, however. We must admit not only that some people might be accidentally incapable of living in an anarchistic society, but, on the contrary, that people are normally not up to this kind of living. We must begin with this realistic assessment. In this area, as well, Christians must be the most realistic of all. Power does not lead people to wickedness; rather, people want to be slaves and get rid of the problems of living by turning them over to power. As they make this capitulation, they discover others' appetite for power. The desire to surrender oneself and the will to power are precisely correlated. Anarchism must be proclaimed in this very real situation. Here, too, comes the word of hope: "In spite of everything, in spite of this human reality, we want to destroy power." *This is Christian hope in politics.*

Most certainly, however, this hope cannot suffice. We must face human evil: not moral evil, which consists of disobeying the present moral code, but *this evil*, a sickness unto death, which leads a person to be a slave and a tyrant. Faced with this evil, we have only two options. Either we organize a repressive system, putting each person in his place, establishing standards of conduct, punishing whoever oversteps the boundaries of the tiny freedom assigned to him. In this case we justify the power of the state. Or we can work for the transformation of humanity (Christians will call this "conversion"), so that people become capable of living with others, serving them, as an expression of freedom. This is the expression of Christian love, the love manifested in Jesus Christ by God, who is on humanity's side.

Anarchists have understood the need for this transformation perfectly. They hoped for it to come about through education, but surely this remedy is insufficient. The anarchist unionists hoped to achieve it through the practice of struggle. By combating power, people develop human qualities: virtue, courage, solidarity, loyalty. Furthermore, the struggle must be waged with virtuous arms: truth, justice, authenticity (and I would happily add another: nonviolence). Otherwise, the struggle would corrupt the combatant, instead of preparing him to enter the anarchist fraternity.

The greats of the movement—V. Griffuelhes, Merrheim, E. Pouget, etc.—understood this point perfectly: education and struggle form the new humanity. True, but we need a deeper motivation. These two pedagogical methods need rooting in something more basic. A more fundamental conversion is required, on the basis of which the rest becomes possible; it would enable people to keep up their courage in the midst of failure. Herein lies the role of the gospel for anarchists. It attests that the possibility of freedom still exists, even for the flabbiest, most servile person, or, on the contrary, for the most tyrannical or swaggering—all those who would seem incapable of any change whatsoever. For this person, whether slave or tyrant, is also loved by God in Jesus Christ, and thus is not beyond the possibility of living in the truth God reveals to us.

I believe this two-edged Christian contribution of realism and hope to be essential for anarchism. Anarchism's need for Christianity shows the possibility of a practical harmony, which could accompany the clear agreement of the two on the theoretical level. This possibility contrasts with the fundamental contradiction of Christianity and Marxism, and the extraordinary uselessness of cooperation between them. I must clarify, however, that in this essay I am not trying to find a new concordism. I do not mean to imply that anarchist thought expresses the Christian political orientation, nor that Christians should adopt an anarchist orientation. In other words, we must not fall into the same error with anarchism that has been made with respect to Marxism!

I have tried to show, contrary to what is usually believed, (1) that no radical contradiction exists between anarchism and the concrete consequences of Christian faith in the sociopolitical area, whereas there is a contradiction between Marxism and the implications of the faith; (2) that anarchism does not imply, as Marxism does, the elimination of Christian specificity; (3) finally, that within the context of modern society and our concrete historical situation, the determining and decisive problem is that of the universal power of the state. We must therefore aim at that problem, which we can do, thanks to anarchism, whereas Communism has shown itself incapable of responding to this challenge. On the contrary, each time it comes to power, it merely reinforces the state.

Refusing a synthesis of Christianity and Marxism does not amount to "preaching submission" (M. Sevegrand, *Le Monde*, Dec. 1978). On the contrary, it means entering a *different* revolutionary way, another way of questioning that is infinitely more radical and profound. Marxist Christianity thwarts and sterilizes this other way, for it means genuine conformism to this world.

Works by the Same Author

(in order of their first publication, usually in French)

I. HISTORY

Etude sur l'évolution et la nature juridique du Mancipium (thesis). Bordeaux: Delmas, 1936.

"Essai sur le recrutement de l'armée française aux XVIe et XVIIe siècles." Académie des Sciences Morales et Politiques' prize, 1941. Apparently never published.

"Introduction à l'histoire de la discipline des Eglises réformées de France." Manuscript which awarded Ellul the "Agrégation" degree at the University of Paris Law Faculty, 1943. Apparently never published.

Histoire des institutions. Vols. I-II: *L'Antiquité;* Vol. III: *Le Moyen Age;* Vol. IV: *XVIe-XVIIIe Siècle;* Vol. V: *Le XIXe Siècle.* Paris: Presses Universitaires de France, 1955-1980.

Histoire de la propagande. 2d ed. Paris: Presses Universitaires de France, 1976.

II. SOCIOLOGY

The Technological Society. Trans. John Wilkinson. New York: Knopf, 1964; London: Jonathan Cape, 1965.

Propaganda: The Formation of Men's Attitudes. Trans. Konrad Kellen and Jean Lerner. New York: Knopf, 1965.

The Political Illusion. Trans. Konrad Kellen. New York: Knopf, 1967; New York: Random House, 1972.

A Critique of the New Commonplaces. Trans. Helen Weaver. New York: Knopf, 1968.

Métamorphose du bourgeois. Paris: Calmann-Lévy, 1967.

Autopsy of Revolution. Trans. Patricia Wolf. New York: Knopf, 1971.

Jeunesse délinquante: Une expérience en province. With Yves Charrier. 2d ed. Nantes: AREFPPI, 1985.

De la révolution aux révoltes. Paris: Calmann-Lévy, 1972.

The New Demons. Trans. C. Edward Hopkin. New York: Seabury, 1975; London: Mowbrays, 1975.

The Betrayal of the West. Trans. Matthew J. O'Connell. New York: Seabury, 1978.

The Technological System. Trans. Joachim Neugroschel. New York: Continuum, 1980.

L'Empire du non-sens: L'Art et la société technicienne. Paris: Presses Universitaires de France, 1980.

The Humiliation of the Word. Trans. Joyce Main Hanks. Grand Rapids: Eerdmans, 1985.

Changer de révolution: L'Inéluctable Prolétariat. Paris: Seuil, 1982.

FLN Propaganda in France during the Algerian War. Trans. Randal Marlin. Ottawa: By Books, 1982.

Le Bluff Technologique. Paris: Hachette, 1988.

III. THEOLOGY

The Theological Foundation of Law. Trans. Marguerite Wieser. Garden City, NY: Doubleday, 1960; London: SCM, 1960; New York: Seabury, 1969.

The Presence of the Kingdom. Trans. Olive Wyon. Philadelphia: Westminster, 1951; London: SCM, 1951; New York: Seabury, 1967.

The Judgment of Jonah. Trans. Geoffrey W. Bromiley. Grand Rapids: Eerdmans, 1971.

Money and Power. Trans. LaVonne Neff. Downers Grove, IL: InterVarsity Press, 1984.

False Presence of the Kingdom. Trans. C. Edward Hopkin. New York: Seabury, 1972.

To Will and To Do: An Ethical Research for Christians. Trans. C. Edward Hopkin. Philadelphia: Pilgrim Press, 1969.

The Politics of God and the Politics of Man. Trans. Geoffrey W. Bromiley. Grand Rapids: Eerdmans, 1972.

Violence: Reflections from a Christian Perspective. Trans. Cecelia Gaul Kings. New York: Seabury, 1969; London: SCM, 1970; London: Mowbrays, 1978.

The Meaning of the City. Trans. Dennis Pardee. Grand Rapids: Eerdmans, 1970.

Prayer and Modern Man. Trans. C. Edward Hopkin. New York: Seabury, 1970.

Hope in Time of Abandonment. Trans. C. Edward Hopkin. New York: Seabury, 1973.

Apocalypse: The Book of Revelation. Trans. George W. Schreiner. New York: Seabury, 1977.

The Ethics of Freedom. Trans. and ed. Geoffrey W. Bromiley. Grand Rapids: Eerdmans, 1976; London: Mowbrays, 1976. The French version, *Ethique de la liberté,* published by Labor et Fides (Geneva), contains some material not included in the English version. This is especially true of the third and final volume, entitled *Les Combats de la liberté* (1984).

Living Faith: Belief and Doubt in a Perilous World. Trans. Peter Heinegg. San Francisco: Harper and Row, 1983.

The Subversion of Christianity. Trans. Geoffrey W. Bromiley. Grand Rapids: Eerdmans, 1985.

Conférence sur l'Apocalypse de Jean. Nantes: AREFPPI, 1985.

Un chrétien pour Israël. Monaco: Editions du Rocher, 1986.

Ce que je crois. Paris: Grasset & Fasquelle, 1987 (soon to be published in English by Eerdmans).

La Raison d'être: Méditation sur l'Ecclésiaste. Paris: Seuil, 1987 (soon to be published in English by Eerdmans).

IV. BOOK-LENGTH JOURNAL ARTICLES

"De la signification des relations publíques dans la société technicienne: Un cas de passage de l'information à la propagande." *L'Année Sociologique,* 3d series (1963), 69-152.

"Impressions d'Israël." *Foi et Vie,* 76, no. 4 (Aug. 1977), 1-72.

"Le Travail." *Foi et Vie,* 79, no. 4 (July 1980), 1-50, 63-86. This is actually a group of articles, most of which are pseudonymous.

V. AUTOBIOGRAPHY

Perspectives on Our Age: Jacques Ellul Speaks on His Life and Work. Ed. William H. Vanderburg. Trans. Joachim Neugroschel. Toronto: Canadian Broadcasting Corp., 1981; New York: Seabury, 1981.

In Season, Out of Season: An Introduction to the Thought of Jacques Ellul: Based on Interviews by Madeleine Garrigou-Lagrange. Trans. Lani K. Niles. San Francisco: Harper and Row, 1982.

Index of Names and Subjects

Christianity: and anarchism, 153-77; and the bourgeoisie, 161; Catholic, 29, 32, 33, 40; and the Communist Party, 57; and conformism, 2, 3-4, 12, 13-14, 21-22, 31-32, 177; and dialectic, 63, 125; and ideology, 1-3, 5, 12, 13-14, 35-36, 49, 51-52, 126- 27; and justice, 6, 10, 37; and Latin America, 151; and K. Marx, 2-3, 12-13, 30, 39, 40-42, 52, 60, 95, 153, 161; and Marxism, 5-14, 21-24, 26-42, 47-57, 59, 62-64, 80, 124-33, 135- 46, 149, 155-57, 173, 176-77; and materialism, 7-8, 12-13, 39-41, 55-56, 144; and moralism, 2; and politics, 22, 29, 31, 33, 37-39, 42, 56, 62, 70, 72, 136, 138, 141-44, 149, 150, 154, 156-75; and the poor, 22, 28, 120-22, 127, 135-36, 142-44; and practice, 6-8, 10, 13, 28-29, 30, 31, 39, 43, 62-63, 65, 69, 72, 74, 88, 124-25, 127-35, 143-45, 146, 173; and preaching, 43, 66-70, 73, 175-76; Protestant, 37-38; and realism, 175-76; and religion, 160, 161; and Resistance, 11-12, 13, 38-39; and revolution, 49-50, 137-40, 146, 148; and the social order, 14, 29; and socialism, 11, 13, 22, 30, 36, 50-51, 53, 139, 140-41, 154-55; specificity of, 14, 31, 35, 48, 50, 136, 139, 154, 173, 177; and J. Stalin, 129; and systems, 2, 20, 51; and technique, 82; and violence, 22. *See also Church*
Church: and anarchism, 155-56, 159-62, 171; as community, 9; criticized, 155, 157, 160-62; diversity of, 49; fragility of, 51; and heresy, 38, 171; history of, 51, 141-43, 160-62, 166-67, 171; and Nazism, 32, 35, 37-38; and the poor, 6, 127, 135, 142; as a power, 6, 141, 160-62, 171; and primitive Christianity, 155, 160- 62, 169-70; and state, 172. *See also* Christianity

Class, social: as determinative, 120, 121, 123, 126-27; existence of, 79, 104-105, 120, 143, 145; and history, 143; and interpretation, 79-84, 120; and K. Marx, 105, 126, 127, 143, 144; struggle, 15, 16, 38, 48, 54, 55, 56-57, 93, 97-98, 105, 107, 114, 120-21, 126-31, 133, 142, 143-46
Clévenot, Michel, 85
Colonialism: and imperialism, 57-60. *See also* Freedom, Indochina, Revolution
Communist Party: appeal of, 18-19, 21, 54, 122; and Christianity, 57; evolution of, 16-18; French, 16, 18-19; and the poor, 131; and practice, 137-39; structures of, 23, 39. *See also* Marxism
Conformism: among Christians, 2, 3-4, 12, 13-14, 21-22, 31-32, 177; and ideology, 2, 3-4, 12, 13-14, 21-22, 31-32, in theology, 96-97; to the world, 3, 49, 177
Creation: in anarchism, 159-60; biblical, 34, 55; and the Kingdom, 62; and Marxism, 41, 55
Cuba, 139, 140, 147-48
Czechoslovakia, 7, 16, 31, 37-38, 148

Daix, P., 12, 15
Deleuze, G., 26
Dhoquois, G. le, 100, 102
Dialectic: biblical, 89, 91, 124-25; in Christianity, 63, 125; in Marxism, 19, 23, 42, 63, 125; practice and theory, 6-7
Dostoyevski, F., 112
Dumas, A., 121 n. 3, 144, 156 n. 2

Ellenstein, Jean, 12, 62-63, 121 n. 4
Ellul, Jacques, works: *Apocalypse: The Book of Revelation,* 169 n. 13; *The Presence of the Kingdom,* 34 n. 10, 50, 119 n. 2

23, 25, 51; and terrorism, 22-25; and theology, 26-36, 118, 128-30, 144; and totalitarianism, 13, 23, 35; values in, 17, 39; and violence, 23, 42, 140, 147; and work, 140. *See also* L. Althusser, Class, Communist Party, Karl Marx, Proletariat

Materialism: and the Bible, 7-8, 40-41, 55, 64, 65, 84-87, 91-94, 97-118, 137, 148-49; and the bourgeoisie, 19, 97; and Christianity, 7-8 , 12-13, 39-41, 55-56, 144; defined, 97-98, 116-17, 119; and God, 55, 97-98; and history, 97-101; and idealism, 55, 111, 117; as irrational, 12-13; and Jesus Christ, 115-16; and the Kingdom, 114; and K. Marx, 12-13, 40, 41, 55, 91, 94, 97, 98, 101, 117, 119; in Marxism, 15, 19, 40, 54-58, 62, 101, 119, 127, 144; and spiritualism, 7-8, 55, 98; and theology, 10, 26-27, 40-41, 75, 111-12, 118-19, 144, 148-49

Mounier, E., 146

Nazism: and the Church, 32, 35, 37-38; as ideology, 4, 35; and Mussolini, 32; and National Socialism, 32

Nietzsche, F.: and F. Belo, 93-95; and Christianity, 2-3; and K. Marx, 94-95

Paul: on "flesh," 8; on Jesus Christ, 62; and practice, 132-33; structure in, 132-33. *See also* Bible

Péguy, Charles, 32-33

Philipp, A., 37

Poland, 7, 16

Politics: and action, 28, 121; and the Bible, 7, 86, 88-90, 103- 15, 124, 137, 157, 163-72; and Christianity, 22, 29, 31, 33, 37- 39, 42, 56, 62, 70, 72, 136, 138, 141-44, 149, 150, 154, 156-75; and freedom, 46-47, 57-59;

and Jesus Christ, 48, 64-68, 112-15, 138, 150, 166-68; and the Kingdom, 136, 166, 168; and Marxism, 31, 33, 56, 62, 120, 126, 138; in theology, 37, 46-48, 59, 60, 67-68, 135, 151, 166-67

Poor: and Christianity, 22, 28, 120-22, 127, 135-36, 142-44; and the church, 6, 127, 135, 142; and the Communist Party, 131; defined, 145; dignity of, 43; and history, 10, 33, 142-43; and Jesus Christ, 10, 28, 44, 56, 89, 110, 112, 120, 122, 136, 137, 142, 145, 167-68; and Marxism, 6, 28, 31, 42, 121-22, 137, 142, 143, 145-47; as priests, 44; and revolution, 139, 142, 145-46, 147; and socialism, 122, 154; and theology, 44, 45, 56, 60, 66, 80, 120, 126, 149. *See also* Poverty, Proletariat

Poverty: and the Bible, 22, 69, 92, 106-107, 145; and Communism, 6; and faith, 28; among workers, 16. *See also* Poor, Theology

Practice, praxis: and the Bible, 132-37, 141; and Christianity, 6-8, 10, 13, 28-29, 30, 31, 39, 43, 62-63, 65, 69, 72, 74, 88, 124-25, 127-35, 143-45, 146, 173; and the Communist Party, 137- 39; and dialectic, 6-7; and faith, 7, 43, 62-63, 133-37, 141, 144; and history, 141, 144-45; and Jesus Christ, 65-66, 69, 73, 87, 110, 114, 122, 130, 132-34, 136, 141, 144; and K. Marx, 101-102, 115, 129-30, 131-33, 143-44; and Marxism, 7-8, 13, 29, 30, 39, 63, 127-31, 137, 142, 148; and Paul, 132-33; and politics, 28, 121; and speech, 43, 65-66, 70, 87; and theology, 124-35

Prayer, 73-75

Presuppositions: in F. Belo, 117; in biblical interpretation, 76-84, 93-94, 96-98; in G. Casalis, 121-23; in R. Chapuis, 26-29; and faith, 60-

Index of Scripture References

OLD TESTAMENT

NEW TESTAMENT